ALL IN THE FAMILY

H144/02

By the same author:
For all the Family
More for all the Family
Teaching the Families
Reaching the Families
Family Worship
Twenty Questions on Baptism
Prayers for all the Family
Drama for all the Family

All in the Family

Edited by
MICHAEL BOTTING

KINGSWAY PUBLICATIONS
EASTBOURNE

The front cover illustration was provided by
Mrs Ruth End.

ISBN 0 85476 546 8

Designed and produced by
Bookprint Creative Services
P.O. Box 827, BN21 3YJ, England for
KINGSWAY PUBLICATIONS LTD
Lottbridge Drove, Eastbourne, E. Sussex BN23 6NT.
Printed in Finland.

This book is dedicated to Bishop Michael and Mrs Myrtle Baughen in recognition of their warm friendship to my wife Mary and me over forty years; and their fellowship in the gospel, especially over the past eleven years in the Diocese of Chester, where I have been very privileged to serve as Joint Director of Lay Training, and for their generous Forewords to two of my books relating to family worship.

Contents

Foreword

I am both pleased and privileged to contribute to Michael Botting's latest book. It comes in a line of invaluable resources, of which he has been the editor, which are concerned with getting the Christian message across. This in itself is an indication of the author's own commitment to evangelism based on carefully prepared material. It is also an indication of his own good practice, which I came to admire as a colleague, of making sure that good ideas are put down on paper and worked out in detail. His illustrations, often by means of overhead projector, are always of high quality, both in conception and execution. 'One in the eye is worth two in the ear', says the proverb, and Michael would certainly agree, aiming whenever possible at both eye and ear.

Michael is concerned with inclusive worship, which means that those of all ages and mental ability will together be able to find some meaning. He aims to restore the balance between teaching occasions when segregation takes place and those where the learning experience is enhanced for everyone by being all together.

In the main part of this book Michael has gathered together a wonderful variety of material, including helpful readings and suggested hymns, based on the Christian seasons and festivals. Those using the outlines will be aware of their own need to plan and prepare thoroughly—particularly in the case of the drama and the visual aids—and hopefully will revise and rewrite the material to suit their own situations. To get the most out of this book will require a good deal of team effort.

I share Michael's enthusiasm for the use of stories, and was challenged to think how I might use the ones he includes in his Appendix. I was reminded too of a book called *The Teaching Methods of Jesus* by Douglas S. Hubery, which suggests criteria from Jesus' own story-telling that should be applied in choosing or even writing stories: Are they credible? Are they interesting? Do they encourage the exercise of the imagination? Is there an element of surprise and a twist in the tale? Do they speak for themselves? I hold the view that true stories are the best stories.

I commend *All in the Family* as a compilation of resource material gathered by someone with vast experience as parish priest and as Diocesan Director of Adult Education and Training, and who knows what he is looking for. My prayer is that the book will help us both to fulfil the command in Habbakuk 2:2: 'Write down the vision, inscribe it on tablets, ready for a herald to carry it with speed'; and also the word of Jesus in Luke 8:8: 'If you have ears to hear, then hear.'

† *Frank Sargeant*
Bishop at Lambeth
December 1995

Introduction

Over recent years another title to replace 'Family Service' has become increasingly popular, namely 'All-Age Worship', and it does have especially in its favour that people who are widowed, divorced or separated, who are lone parents or who have never been married, no longer feel marginalised. Jackie Cray, in her recent book *Seen and Heard* (Monarch, 1995), refers to this very group and writes how they 'are keenly aware of the ways in which their day-to-day experience differs from the cosy perfection of the families in the TV commercials. For them the word "family" gives a very clear message: "Not you!"' (p 33).

Whether we call it a Family Service or All-Age Worship what should be its distinguishing features? I suggest there are five:

It must include everyone

It is *not* a children's service, though of course children must essentially be part of it. Jackie Cray devotes a chapter to 'A Biblical View of Family and Children' in her book quoted above. Mrs Cray acknowledges that 'even if we wanted to, we couldn't recreate the conditions in which those long-ago extended families lived and thrived' (p 30). However, she points out that

both Old and New Testaments picture children growing up in a variety of family situations, most of them large-scale, all of them covering several generations. To experience family life was to experience community. When Jesus founded his church he called everybody into a renewed experience of community. In the church we never stop being individuals, but if we are to be the community God intends us to be, we have to learn to let go of some of our twentieth-century *individualistic* attitudes (p 41).

This may mean that some adults in our congregations need educating about the presence of children in the service. They are not just to be tolerated, possibly reluctantly, but generously accepted as having as much right to be there as anyone else.

To be practical, however, I believe that if it is at all possible there ought to be a creche for, say, the under threes, and perhaps also a special group for the three to fives. Even in the best planned services it will be difficult to keep the attention of such young children, with the consequence that their parents will be more concerned with keeping them quiet than sharing in any realistic way in worship.

I make no apology in advocating the principle of having a service that caters for the 'nuclear family'. From what is said above, especially by Mrs Cray, I know the reality is often very different, but the Family/All-Age Service is intended to help families stay together.

It has been reckoned that 80% of families rarely meet: shift work, TV and microwave ovens discourage meals being eaten together. Lord Coggan was complaining over thirty years ago that the church seemed bent on dividing families rather than uniting them, with so many sectional groups. Jackie Cray makes the same complaint (p 33). Therefore, every attempt must be made to include the whole church household: married and single, widowed, separated and divorced, teenagers and children.

No one should be patronised, but if questions are being put to the congregation, say during a quiz or in the talk, it may be appropriate to indicate from which age group an answer is expected.

There must be teaching appropriate for everyone

I believe that the opportunity to teach the Christian faith must still be an important element in the Family/All-Age Service, but for many churches this may be the main service of the day, not only attended by all biological ages, but also all spiritual ages. For this reason a varied pattern for different Sundays of the month seems essential. On one Sunday (preferably the first, so that it is easily remembered), all ages above five remain in church, and the whole service is designed to cater for all. On other Sundays children should have their own classes for most of the time and only be in the main worship area for part of the service. This enables the adults to receive a biblical exposition geared at their level.

So when should the children be in? In many churches it is often at the most inappropriate time at the beginning, when they may have to endure what is essentially adult worship including a long hymn, Confession, a Psalm, Canticle and possibly two lessons! There is much to be said for everyone going to their own groups at the beginning: the children to their classes and adults into church. Then the children can join their parents towards the end of the morning worship. Adults have a service similar in content to ASB Rite A Communion Service to the end of the creed. There is then music while the children join their parents, followed by a short act of worship that can include two sung items, a special activity, and prayers, perhaps read by a family. When the service is Holy Communion older children can join their parents at The Peace.

It should be a 'bridge' service

Thirty years ago when I first began a Family Service the fringe of the church was somewhat larger, though bishops like Gavin Reid of Maidstone and John Finney of Pontefract tell us that some fringe still exists. General Synod's *All God's Children?* (NS/CHP) reveals that the church only has contact with 15% of the country's children, which means that we can no longer assume a Sunday school background for most adults—something which I could take for granted in 1962. However, while there is some fringe I believe we should exploit it for the Lord and the Family/All-Age Service can be one means. People still want to have their children baptised or their Banns called. This service is the obvious setting, especially if it is the one where most of the children are in for the whole time.

Uniformed organisations like Scouts and Guides still exist, so they can continue to be encouraged to parade monthly.

Because of the hope that there will be those present unfamiliar with worship, they must be helped to find their way around with minimum embarrassment. Full use should be made of modern facilities to produce service sheets. More and more churches have word processors and there is much Christian software available, such as *Worship Master* from Hodder and OUP.

It should be a liturgical service

Since Family/All-Age Services have spread so far and wide the Liturgical Commission has recently produced

A Service of the Word which has made such services legal, and honest men of the bishops and clergy who have unofficially permitted them for years. This is not a liturgy as such, but rather outlines what such services must contain, namely: a recognisable beginning and ending, a Confession and Creed, Intercessions, at least one Lesson from Scripture and a sermon. I have attended a number of Family Services in different locations in my time, either on holiday or as visiting preacher or both. Some have been nothing more than Matins with some choruses and a two-minute thought for children. At one church the vicar was introducing a Family Service for the first time. He rightly chose Harvest for the occasion, but we sang no harvest hymns, had a competition that went on for ten minutes with prizes for all and a twelve-minute anthem from the choir, though I'm not sure in what language. I finally reached the pulpit fifty-five minutes after the service began!

At the other extreme I preached at a service where there was no obvious beginning, because choruses were being sung fifteen minutes before the scheduled start and continued some time after. All the songs were new to my wife and me, and we are not unfamiliar with modern songs by Graham Kendrick and others. Hardly a service to commend to those feeling their way into, or back into the church. There was no Confession, Lord's Prayer, Lesson, Creed or Grace! So I gratefully welcome the Liturgical Commission's work, which seeks to remedy these and other horrors by clearly laying down what a Family/All-Age Service must contain, but giving freedom within the framework. Indeed freedom is important. Because the service is liturgical, it does not mean that it should be 'starchy'. There should be reverence, but also flexibility and a relaxed atmosphere, where some humour is not out of place. We are never actually told that Jesus laughed, but he was adept at exaggeration (eg Matthew 7:3–5) and I am sure his audiences frequently found his preaching very funny.

The worship model should be clear

In a perceptive article in the *Church Times* in July 1994 Canon Robert Warren, formerly Vicar of St Thomas's, Crookes, Sheffield and now the Church of England's National Officer for Evangelism, described three possible models, which he saw people using to shape worship today. There is *the performance model*, which is best illustrated by our English cathedrals, where most people are audience. Then there is *the spectator-sport model*, which might be called the charismatic model, where the congregation take a more active part, cheering, clapping, singing and responding to what is being done by others up at the front. The third is *the participative drama model*. Canon Warren describes this as follows:

> The worship is a re-enactment of the saving acts of God in which everyone participates and makes present that which has arisen out of the past. In such a model the leader is like the conductor of an orchestra—the only person who does not play an instrument, but draws out the best contributions and the most harmonious. This model links up with the modern scientific model of the universe. Scientists no longer see humankind as objective spectators of a mechanism called creation, but as a participant in the whole process. Subjective and objective, married in science, need to be married in contemporary worship.

This third model, I suggest, splendidly describes exactly what Family/All-Age Worship should be. The purpose of this book is to aim towards that end.

I often get enquiries about two particular problems: first that children prefer their Sunday class meetings to the Family Service. I think the only comment I can offer is that a serious attempt must be made to ensure that there is provision for every age group, and that everyone must accept that Family Services are likely to be noisy! The second problem concerns encouraging people who come to Family Services regularly to make the transition to communicant membership. Ultimately I believe this is a matter of personal pastoral ministry. However I have heard of the Family/All-Age Service being combined regularly with Holy Communion—the earlier part, lasting about forty minutes, having a shape similar to the ASB Ministry of the Word with Intercessions. Those not wishing to take Communion, including most (but not all) of the children, then move to a nearby room or hall for drinks and biscuits, while the rest of the congregation proceed with the Eucharist. Personally I am not enthusiastic about this arrangement, except for major festivals.

There is much to be said for having a team of people to organise the whole service. They should be carefully chosen to include such key people as the leader of the music group, drama group, etc, so that every effort can be made to draw people in to be involved in some way. If drama is not being used, consider how the Lesson might be read by various people taking parts. Such a team *must* be given adequate advanced notice, so that they can plan and pray without undue pressure. Alan Pugmire has written an excellent chapter on teamwork in my book *More for all the Family* (pp 25ff).

In the pages that follow sixty themes have been chosen, under the same headings as in my three previous books of talks. However I have made the Christian year section begin with Creation, in keeping with the Alternative Service Book. I understand that the next Prayer Book being prepared by the Liturgical Commission to replace the ASB in 2000 AD will revert to the Christian year beginning with Advent, but that should not confuse the users of this book for the next four years!

Under each theme will be found suggested material that might be incorporated into a particular act of Family/All-Age Worship. Most of the talks have not been published before, though three of my own appeared in the first edition of *Reaching the Families* (Falcon, 1969).

The majority of the stories have not been published before, and are printed in full. The longer ones, especially those by the Revd Pat Ashe, have been placed in Appendix 1. These might be shortened for church use, but with three to five groups can be used in full.

The suggested dramatic sketches and prayers are from my two books *Drama for all the Family* and *Prayers for all the Family*, unless otherwise stated. Where references to other books are made, authors and publishers are mentioned in Appendix 2.

I have been told by one of my local Christian bookshops that there is a constant demand from school teachers for material for school assemblies. I hope that some of this material will be found suitable in that setting also.

I am delighted that Bishop Frank Sargeant, now Bishop at Lambeth, has so kindly written a Foreword, as well as providing a talk. When he was Bishop of Stockport (1984–94) we worked very closely together in lay training, promoting the Bishop of Chester's course in Christian faith and life. A further delight was that my daughter Ruth has provided the front cover picture, giving an additional meaning to the title of the book!

The United Nations designated 1994 as International Year of the Family. I believe that *every* year should emphasise the importance of the family, as I trust every decade, till Jesus returns, will continue to be one of evangelism. I hope that those reading this book will be encouraged to take a fresh look at their Family/All-Age Worship services, or even to start featuring them, so that under the direction and power of the Holy Spirit these may continue to be growing points in the church's life to the praise and glory of the God and Father of our Lord Jesus Christ.

Michael Botting
Chester 1995

THE CHRISTIAN YEAR

1 God—the Unseen Creator

AIM

To further our understanding of God the Creator.

TEXTS

Genesis 1:1–5; Romans 1:20.

DRAMA/STORY

Either act the following sketch or tell as a story. For an alternative, see *Ten Minute Miracle Plays* (Appendix 2) 'In the beginning', pp 7–10.

Ideally obtain an easily portable model of the solar universe. Alternatively a good quality globe of the world will be adequate.

The scene is a school classroom. TEACHER 1 enters with model or globe and places it on a table up front. TEACHER 2 enters and the following dialogue ensues:

TEACHER 2: Are you doing anything on Sunday morning?

TEACHER 1: Well, yes. I shall be going to church.

TEACHER 2: You surely don't believe all that God nonsense, do you? [*He suddenly notices the model or globe and looks at it intently.*] Who made this? It's beautiful.

TEACHER 1: No one.

TEACHER 2: What do you mean, no one?

TEACHER 1: It just appeared.

TEACHER 2: [*Showing obvious impatience*] Don't be stupid. Someone must have made it.

TEACHER 1: How can you insist that someone must have made this model, when you don't believe anyone made something infinitely greater—the real universe?

HYMNS

Addison's hymn 'The spacious firmament on high'. See also the section in the hymn book on God the Creator.

PRAYERS

Prayers for all the Family 1; 92; 115 (Litany); 124; 125; 335.

MAIN TALK

Preparation

You will need a wooden chair and some simple illustrations, OHP transparencies or large drawings showing (1) a tree; (2) an explosion to superimpose on the tree, or a drawing of an explosion in a tree; (3) furniture; (4) buildings; (5) a bridge; (6) a globe (or an actual globe).

Presentation

The chair is placed in front of the congregation and the talk begins with a question and answer session. What is this? A chair. How do we know it's a chair? Just by looking at it—we can see it's a chair. Do you think this chair is real, or are we just imagining it? Perhaps it isn't really there at all. We can test whether it's real if we think about what it is used for. It's used for sitting on. Sometimes little people may use it to stand on to reach something on a high shelf. Or Mum might stand on it and scream while a mouse enjoys running around underneath [the speaker may like to demonstrate!]. We need somebody to come and try sitting (or standing) on this chair. [Ask one or two people from the congregation to do so.]

Well, the chair seemed real enough when it was tried out. It's good to have a real chair here this morning. Let's think a bit more about it. Has it always been a chair, or did it have to become a chair? It had to become a chair. So what is it made of? It's made of wood. Where does wood come from? It comes from trees. [Show illustration 1.] But how did the wood get from being part of a tree to being a chair? Do you think the tree was struck by lightning, or an explosion blew the tree to bits [show illustration 2] and some of the bits came together to make this chair? Of course not! That would be a rather silly thing to think, wouldn't it?

How then did it become a chair? Did it make itself? No, our intelligence tells us that this chair is a chair because somebody, somewhere made it. We call him a carpenter. Does anyone here today know the carpenter who made this chair? Has anyone ever seen him? No? Well, that's hardly surprising. But because none of us knows or has seen the person who made this chair, it does not mean that person does not exist. It would be impossible for the chair to make itself. It is a chair only because somebody made it.

It is the same with other things that have shape, pattern and purpose. All of them have been made by somebody, somewhere [show illustration 3]. Some things are made by carpenters [illustration 4]. Some things are made by bricklayers and building workers [illustration 5]. Some things are made by engineers. We could go on and on. Everything that has shape, pattern and purpose has been made by somebody, somewhere.

Now let's look beyond things that man has made and think about the world itself [illustration 6]. Our world has shape and order. Things happen in such a regular pattern that we know we can depend on them completely. Day and night follow each other unceasingly. Spring, summer, autumn and winter follow each other each year. Plants grow, produce fruit and seed, die off and new ones grow from the seeds. Out in space, we know that the universe behaves in an orderly way. Planets follow regular orbits and scientists can tell us when exciting things like eclipses are going to happen. The big question is—How did it all happen?

Are the universe and our world only imaginary? [Here the speaker may stamp a foot or even jump up and down.] It seems real enough to me. Has our world always existed? The thinkers—philosophers and scientists—believe that the world and our universe have *not* always existed, but that at some point in time they had a beginning. Did it all happen by chance though, through some explosion or 'Big Bang' of some kind as some scientists would have us believe? Anyone who has seen the results of explosions, even if only by means of pictures on television and in newspapers, could surely never be fooled into believing that the order and regular behaviour of our world could be brought about by a 'Big Bang'. Explosions destroy things and cause chaos, not order.

We know just from thinking about the chair that our world could not have made itself, but must have been made by someone. The Bible tells us that God is the maker of our world. St Paul tells us in his letter to the Christians in Rome: 'Ever since the creation of the world

his invisible nature, namely his eternal power and deity, has been clearly perceived in the things that have been made' (Rom 1:20).

[For this last part of the talk the speaker can either indicate the chair again, or even actually sit on it.]

We may not have seen the person who made this chair, but we know it is real and it has been put together in a particular way to give it a purpose. We may not have seen God, but his handiwork is all around us in the world he made. It has shape, pattern and purpose and we Christians believe it is the work of the creative mind of God.

John Bavin
Forden, Welshpool

2 Man—Unique in God's Creation

Aim

To show that human beings are special and different from everything else created by God.

Text

Genesis 1:26–31.

Drama/Story

Acting Up (Appendix 2) 'In the Beginning', pp 7–10.

Hymns

'All creatures of our God and King'; 'All people that on earth do dwell'. See also the section in the hymn book on God the Creator.

Prayers

Prayers for all the Family 1; 115 (Litany); 124; 125; 335.

Main Talk

Preparation

Prepare simple drawings on OHP acetates or on large sheets of card, as shown.

Presentation

Some years ago a Japanese business man, while on his travels, began reading a Bible which he found in his hotel room. As he read it, he became more and more excited because he found that the story it told was about people just like him. 'This is *my* story,' he said. And before he had finished reading it, he had become a Christian. He was quite right—the Bible is first and foremost the story of people.

If you look at a Bible, you'll see it usually consists of around a thousand pages. Yet it takes only one of those pages to tell about the creation of the sun, moon and stars, the earth, the plants, the fish and the animals. The rest tells the story of people. It's as though everything that happened before people were created was part of the preparation for that moment when they came into being. This alone ought to give us some idea of the importance God placed upon the last of the creatures he made. [This may be an appropriate place to mention a couple of points about Darwin's theory of evolution, namely: (1) A theory is an idea for which there is no actual proof, and there are things which cannot be proved about Darwin's theory. (2) Darwin did *not* say we came from apes or monkeys. He suggested that men and monkeys came from a common stock, which is a different matter. Hens and sparrows are both birds; they come from common stock. But to suggest that hens come from sparrows or vice versa, is laughable.]

We are different from the rest of creation for a number of reasons.

First, when God made Adam he *spoke* to him. [Illustration 1.] God saw that his creation was good, but he never spoke to anything else he made. He never spoke to the sun, the moon or the stars; he never spoke to the planets, the fish or the animals. He spoke to Adam because he was different from everything else he had made. There is one small exception to this that I will deal with shortly. God told men and women to be fruitful and multiply, which means they were to have children so that they could look after the world God had put them in. That brings me to the next point.

God gave the men and women a great *task to perform*— to fill the earth and subdue it. [Illustration 2.] That meant God was putting them in control of the earth. No other creature was given such power over the rest of creation. Now power brings with it something else—responsibility. God expects us to use wisely the power we have been given. When we hear of the way we have polluted the air and the water in rivers, hunted some animals to extinction and destroyed much of the world's natural resources in the quest for wealth, we can only feel sad that we have not been as responsible as we should have been. This is because we do not use our God-given power in the right way all the time. In some versions of the Bible, Adam is not told to fill the earth, but to replenish it. That means we should renew or replace those things we use up and not just use them until they run out or are spoiled.

In giving us this great task, God also gave a *pattern of life* similar to the one he himself followed in creation— namely to work for six days and then to rest for a day. [Illustration 3.] No species of animal lives to our pattern of life—not even the apes and monkeys.

God spoke to Adam and we know that Adam was allowed to speak to God. God brought the animals and birds to him to 'see what he would call them, and whatever the man called every living creature, that was its name' (Gen 2:19). Adam must have had a lot of fun giving names like 'hippopotamus'! When God walked in the garden in the cool of the day, he called to Adam and Adam answered him. The only time God spoke to any

1.

BE FRUITFUL
AND MULTIPLY

2.

FILL THE EARTH
AND SUBDUE IT

3. WORK SIX DAYS

REST ONE

4.

5.

6.

other creature was to curse the serpent for what it had done, and the serpent was unable to answer God a word. God and man can still speak to each other.

God speaks in various ways—through the Bible, through his servants, through prophecy, sometimes through visions and dreams, and so on. We may still speak to God through prayer [illustration 4]. We also have the ability to worship God, to thank him and to praise him. To pray, to worship, to thank and to praise are special gifts given only to us. Other gifts given only to us are the ability to make music with instruments other than the voice, and to enjoy jokes and laughter.

All of the Bible, except the first page, is the story of people. It has been said that God the Father loved the Son so much he wanted millions more like him. That is why he made so many. When Adam put himself outside the security of God's love by sinning, God went to tremendous lengths to win back the human race. He spent thousands of years making preparations and then, at exactly the right moment in history, he himself became a human being when he sent God the Son to be one of us [illustration 5].

Having lived a perfect life on this earth, God the Son, our Lord Jesus, died a cruel death on the cross [illustration 6] to pay the price of sin and to put us right with God, so that we could once again enjoy the complete security of his love in his company. What lengths God went to for the love of his special creation—men and women.

John Bavin
Forden, Welshpool

3 Dinner for Two—a Harvest Talk

AIM

To look at various ways in which God provides double blessings.

TEXTS

Genesis 1:26–end (especially v 29); 8:22; 2 Corinthians 9: 10–11; John 10:10.

DRAMA

Acting Up (Appendix 2) 'Harvest Gifts', pp 66–67.

STORY

A man once had two similar dreams in one night. In the first he realised he was in hell. Lots of people were all sitting round a vast table laden with wonderful food, but they were all starving. The reason was that they had long spoons and forks attached to their arms, which prevented them from getting any of the delicious food to their mouths. The dream faded.

In the next dream the man realised he was obviously in heaven. There was the same table laden with food and all the people had these long spoons and forks attached to their arms, but they were all very happy and well fed.

How?

They all fed one another!

Hymn

Select from Harvest section of hymn book.

Prayers

Prayers for all the Family 94; 107 (Litany Harvest Confession); 119 (Litany Harvest Thanksgiving); 274; 340.

Main Talk

Preparation

Either during the service or before, recruit about six children to help you as cooks or waiters to hold menus. Place among the harvest decorations an apple, a tomato, a melon, an orange, and a plum, kidney bean or any fruit or vegetable which contains a seed.

Prepare the three menu cards illustrated below. The cards will need to be large and should preferably be coloured. The wording must be clearly seen.

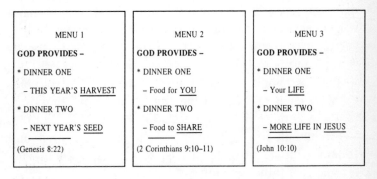

MENU 1	MENU 2	MENU 3
GOD PROVIDES –	**GOD PROVIDES –**	**GOD PROVIDES –**
* DINNER ONE	* DINNER ONE	* DINNER ONE
– THIS YEAR'S HARVEST	– Food for YOU	– Your LIFE
* DINNER TWO	* DINNER TWO	* DINNER TWO
– NEXT YEAR'S SEED	– Food to SHARE	– MORE LIFE IN JESUS
(Genesis 8:22)	(2 Corinthians 9:10–11)	(John 10:10)

Presentation

Ask for volunteer helpers if not already arranged.

Collect up the additions you have made to the harvest decorations.

Demonstrate with the children, by cutting open the fruit and vegetables, that each contains seeds. (The children might be allowed to do some of the cutting, provided there is no danger of them cutting themselves.)

Menu 1 should be held up by Waiter 1. Develop the theme of God's provision of Dinner one, this year's harvest, and Dinner two, next year's seed.

Some food we eat is itself the seed, eg wheat and potatoes, and a part of the harvest must be retained as the 'seed corn'.

Read Genesis 8:22 to emphasise God's promise of his continuing provision.

Menu 2 should be held up by Waiter 2. Use this illustration to emphasise that God's provision is not for us alone. God provides us with Dinner one, food for ourselves. Even in towns we should remember that without the harvest there would be no McDonald's, cheese and onion crisps or fish and chips.

What we receive in our affluent society also requires us to use our resources to provide Dinner two, that is to share with others who may have no harvest to celebrate.

Read 2 Corinthians 9:10–11 to show that God expects us to share his gifts.

Menu 3 should be held up by Waiter 3. God has provided each of us with the life we are now enjoying, but there is more in our Father's love for us.

Our human life is Dinner one, a gift from God our Creator. But he also desires us to be his children and become like him (see Genesis 1:26).

In Jesus, Dinner two, we can have life in all its fullness, both here and now and for ever. Quote Jesus' words from John 10:10.

Recap: God, our loving heavenly Father provides double blessings:

- Harvest for this year AND seed for the next
- Food for us AND food to share
- Life to live AND more life in Jesus.

In fact—Dinner for Two.

Ron Sutton
Macclesfield

4   Sharing the Harvest

AIM

To show our responsibility to share both material things and spiritual truths.

TEXT

John 6:27–36.

DRAMA

Drama for all the Family 47 'Fresh Bread'.

STORY

'Toy Soldier Loses His Busby' (Appendix 1.A).

HYMNS

Select from Harvest section of hymn book.

PRAYERS

Prayers for all the Family 94; 107 (Litany Harvest Confession); 119 (Litany Harvest Thanksgiving); 274; 340; 403.

Main Talk

Preparation

Either on OHP acetates or large pieces of card, write the following words—one on each card:

> harvest, earth, vast, have, eat, save, trash, hearts, hear, starve, share

(All of these can be produced from the letters of 'harvest'.)

Presentation

1. Talk about word games and their popularity.
You may want to set up a competition for words from the letters HARVEST, maybe for a harvest supper game. At our church someone managed 200!
Display the word 'harvest'.
Pick out a few examples of words that can be made from these letters.

2. Draw people's attention to the harvest produce. We thank God for the fruits of the EARTH. [Show the card with 'earth' on it.)

3. We thank God that our harvest is VAST (show word). We have so much—food, houses, possessions, health, clothing, friendship.

4. Divide the world into those who have and those who have not. We are surely those who HAVE (show word). We praise God.

5. We have plenty to EAT (show word). Most of us have no worries about where our next meal will come from. We may not be rich, but we mostly have more than sufficient.

6. In fact many of us have enough so that we can SAVE (show word). We have more than enough.

7. We are very wasteful with food and other resources. We create TRASH (show word). (Perhaps mention the Green movement.)

8. Harvest is a time when we can thank God from the bottom of our HEARTS (show word).

9. But we must be blind or deaf not to realise there are many who do not have food, security, safety, health. We probably don't know them, but we do see them and HEAR (show word) about them.

10. While we eat and drink and enjoy our harvest, there are many who STARVE (show word), and we pray for them.

11. It is a fact that the earth is capable of producing enough for everyone's need (but not greed). We must be willing to SHARE (show word), perhaps by adjusting our lifestyle.

12. All this is about material things but in the reading Jesus talks of spiritual food. The same principles apply. We HAVE, others STARVE. We must SHARE the gospel message.

Paul Day
Loughborough

5 Perfect Gifts

AIM

To ensure that we recognise what God has provided, and are truly thankful.

TEXT

James 1:17.

DRAMA

Drama for all the Family No 41 'Love is . . .'.
Scenes and Wonders (Appendix 2) p 21 'Give and Take'.

STORY

'Camelot Learns to Say Thank You' (Appendix 1.B).

HYMNS

Select from Harvest section of hymn book. A suitable concluding hymn would be, 'I do not know what lies ahead', *Youth Praise* 102.

PRAYERS

See those mentioned in Talk 3. For Friends see *Prayers for all the Family* 98; 146; 411. For further Thanksgivings see Section 1, Chapters 4 and 5 of that book.

MAIN TALK

Preparation

Make three self-standing three-dimensional outsize cardboard containers and place them at the front in advance of the talk. The first should contain a large fruit or vegetable, the third a large calendar. The second should be large enough to hold a small child (known to at least some in church) to be hidden inside during, say, the hymn preceding the talk. Label them 'Food', 'Friends' and 'Future'.

Presentation

1. FOOD

Focus on the first carton. We tend to take daily food for granted. The truth is that when we have done all that is necessary—sowing, reaping, cooking, storing, packaging, distributing, consuming—still, originally and ultimately, we are totally dependent upon the Giver of every good and perfect gift. And his provision is perfect (see Genesis 8:22; Matthew 6:25ff).

Produce the fruit or vegetable from the first carton and read James 1:17.

2. FRIENDS

Friends can also be taken too much for granted. God has created us to relate to each other, but human sinfulness disrupts, divides and destroys. Human friendship is meant to be cultivated and valued. Regrettably it is often deeply undervalued.

Produce the child from inside the carton. Ask him/her who his/her friends are, and why (this may need a little preparation so as to be as natural as possible).

Remind everyone of:

(a) Proverbs 18:24—the 'Friend who sticks closer than a brother'.

(b) Matthew 11:19—the 'Friend of sinners'.

(c) James 2:23—'God's friend'.

God offers us spiritual new life through his word (Jas 1:18).

We are his friends for ever through the love he has shown us in the death and resurrection of Jesus.

3. FUTURE

Focus on the third carton. The gift of eternal life in Christ means we are heirs together of an assured future: 'As I was . . . so I will be' (Josh 1:5).

Produce the large calendar from inside the carton. The future is largely unknown to us, but known and planned by God to perfection: 'Every good and perfect gift . . . from the Father . . . Who does not change like shifting shadows.'

Conclusion

We know that where mankind is involved so much is imperfect—in provision, in friendship, in our attitude to the future. We must lift our spiritual sights, and place our trust in God.

Garth Grinham
Douglas, Isle of Man

6 Harvest

AIM

To tell a Harvest story with a sense of mission, based on Jesus' Parable of the Sower.

TEXTS

Matthew 13:1–23; Mark 4:1–20; Luke 8:4–15.

DRAMA

Drama for all the Family 28 'The Jam Factory'.

HYMNS

Select from the Harvest section of the hymn book.

PRAYERS

Prayers for all the Family 94; 107 (Litany Harvest Confession); 119 (Litany Harvest Thanksgiving); 223; 231; 274; 340; 341.

MAIN TALK

Presentation

There were once four seeds. Their names were Proceed, Supersede, Concede and Succeed.

47

They lived in a sack in the corner of a barn. In winter they huddled together and talked about what they would do when the spring came bringing warm weather, and the time for them to be planted. They hoped they would grow into long stalks of wheat.

And they were all different.

Proceed was on the top of the pile. When the time came to be planted she jumped, but she jumped too far and landed on the path, and was helpless. A farmer walking along the path on his way home trod on her, and a bird came to eat her for his dinner.

Supersede had ambitions. He bounced on to some rocky ground and, being energetic, dug in and began to grow. He soon grew a large stalk, but his roots were not strong enough, as they could not get down into the hard ground. He died of a combination of thirst and frustration.

Concede had worries. She was always bothered about something. She worried whether she'd do as well as the others. Would she be as tall or as golden brown? To make herself feel good she chose a weed as a friend. She knew it was dangerous because wheat and weeds are enemies. Weeds are not to be trusted because they take the seeds' food. They take all the goodness and moisture from the ground. She died of starvation: some say choked by the weed.

Succeed was trusting, kind and patient. He trusted God to send rain for drink and warmth from the sun to make him stand up straight. He landed in deep soil, put down his roots and grew and grew and grew. He grew 100 seeds as he developed.

As Christians we are like the four seeds growing up for God, our heavenly Father.

Like *Proceed* we must be enthusiastic, but we must realise that it does not all depend upon us. Jesus is with us to help and support us, and we must not overstretch ourselves.

The lesson of *Supersede* is: 'Don't try to do too much too quickly or you will get disheartened.' Get the right kind of nourishment. You will need prayer, and Bible strength, and the support of other Christians.

There is another lesson—don't appear to be so strong yourself that you overwhelm other people. They may need gentle handling, and some will need support because they are lonely or sad or hurt. Some will have lost touch with the church. Some will never have been to church and some will never have heard the good news of Jesus.

Then there is the lesson from *Concede*. Be careful how you use your time and energy. A lot of time can be wasted because you are in the wrong place with the wrong people. It may be a hard thing to say but Jesus was quite definite when he sent his disciples out. He said, 'If you are not welcome, move on' (Lk 10).

Let's pray that we will be like *Succeed* who found the right place to be; that we will be the seed of the good news of Jesus who died on the cross for us. He said, 'Truly, truly, I say to you, unless a grain of wheat falls into the earth and dies, it remains alone; but if it dies it bears much fruit' (Jn 12:24). That is the Christian seed which God plants in his earth. He blesses it and brings the harvest.

As we thank him in our Harvest Thanksgiving for the good things he gives us, to keep us alive and help us to grow, so we thank him for the harvest of Jesus' death and resurrection and for the gifts of his Holy Spirit. We thank him for the harvest of Christians throughout the world, who themselves become the seeds—you and I—who have to be scattered to bring others to Jesus as Lord and Saviour.

Frank Sargeant
Bishop at Lambeth

7 God's Light
A Service for All Saints' Tide

AIM

To show that God's light is more important than Hallo-we'en.

TEXT/DRAMA/HYMNS/PRAYERS

All are incorporated in the service outline that follows.

Preparation

Four different age groups should rehearse in Sunday school or on previous occasions.

Group 1: three- to five-year-olds

These should preferably wear white, for example Christmas angel costumes, and should carry stars on sticks. They should hide under a black curtain, or behind a clothes rack covered by a black cloth on one side and a white sheet on the other. During the reading from Genesis 1:1–5 the children jump up at 'and there was light'. Alternatively adults can move the rack round behind the children with the white side showing.

Group 2: five- to eight-year-olds

These should stumble up the aisle, feeling their way as if in the dark, to the front where there should be a round paper balloon-type light shade over a light on a high stand. White crepe paper streamers are attached to the light shade. When the children reach the stand, the light should be turned on and the children should look happy and take the streamers and move out, as far as the streamers will allow, in a circle. They then shout together, 'Jesus said, "I am the Light of the World!"'

Group 3: eleven- to fourteen-year-olds

These children should mime one-paragraph stories of two or three saints, read by an adult. They can be stories of a biblical, a medieval and a modern saint. The patron saint of the church might be one possibility. Such stories are available from a Ladybird book, or *Seasons, Saints and Sticky Tape* (National Society, Church House Publishing). Actions should be mimed in a stylised way. In between the actions the characters should 'freeze'.

Group 4: eight- to eleven-year-olds

These children should mime helping an old person who has dropped shopping, and helping a blind person across the road. They should then light candles from one person to another and mime talking to each other about Jesus.

Presentation

Introduction   Some people are frightened of the dark: people who don't want to be seen doing wrong act at night. Hallowe'en and 'trick or treat' are meant to frighten. Read John 3:19.

1. GOD'S LIGHT IN CREATION

Reading: Genesis 1:1–5 (Group 1).
Hymn: 'Praise the Lord, ye heavens adore him'.
Song: 'They say he's wonderful'.

2. GOD'S LIGHT IN CHRIST

Reading: Luke 2:27b-32. Comment that Jesus was himself light to a world that was frightened and full of wrong. The old man Simeon sensed this while Jesus was still a baby.

God had promised that he would let other people besides the Jews know about him and the best way to live. We are some of those people.

Song: 'The light of Christ' (Group 2).

Creed

3. GOD'S LIGHT IN THE SAINTS

Introductory comment that God has made himself known through people who have believed in Jesus and have shown that in various ways. Saints are people who believe in Jesus and belong to God's family. When they do wrong they are forgiven because Jesus died for them. God loves us even when we do the worst we can, like killing Jesus, but we have to be sorry for what is wrong and we have to ask for forgiveness. We are all saints if we have asked for that forgiveness and been made God's friends. There are people who are famous because they are so glad to be God's friends that they have done special things for him. Let's hear about some of them (Group 3). Prayers of St Richard and St Ignatius.

Hymn: 'Make me a channel of your peace'.

4. GOD'S LIGHT IN US

Mime: (Group 4).

Song: 'This little light of mine'.

Comment about the dangers of Hallowe'en. All Saints' Day reminds us of the light of God which dispels the darkness of our fears and worries, and the spiritual darkness of the occult. Let's have fun, but let's do it in a way which brings light and happiness. And let's share the happiness which we have because we know God.

Hymn: 'All creatures of our God and King'.

Prayer: 'Lighten our darkness . . .' (the Third Collect from Evening Prayer).

Blessing: Numbers 6:24–26.

Jessie Axtell
Manchester

8 Peace—a Talk for Remembrance Sunday

AIM

To explain that Jesus comes to bring peace, but peace begins with us.

TEXT

Micah 4:1–5.

DRAMA

Drama for all the Family 17 'Happy Families'.

STORY

The Editor, who served in the Royal Artillery during the Second World War, was at Christmas 1944 stationed on the German border in the area of the famous Battle of the Bulge.

His regiment did not know whether the Germans would continue the tradition of ceasing fighting on Christmas Day itself, so the signalmen were on duty in the next room to where the padre was holding a simple service of Morning Prayer with carols. From time to time the worshippers could hear the signalmen indicating how strong a signal they were receiving from various command posts, strength 5 being the strongest.

The padre had, of course, included particular prayers for peace in the service, in view of the emergency situation, and he concluded with the plea 'Lord, hear our prayer.' From the signal post came the reassuring response, 'Hear you strength 5!'

The war in Europe ended five months later.

HYMNS

Traditional Remembrance Sunday hymns, such as 'O God, our help in ages past'. The more recent hymn 'Make me a channel of your peace' would be appropriate.

PRAYERS

Prayers for all the Family 184; 185; 352; 353.

MAIN TALK

Preparation

Make a recording of a baby crying loudly (optional).

Innocent looking toy (eg Duplo) or stick.

Make a 'rapid-fire banger': buy twelve party poppers, drill twelve holes in a line in a piece of wood and fit stems of poppers through the holes so that they fit snugly and firing-strings hang out the other side. Take a long piece of string and join to all the firing strings, so that when pulled, the poppers will go off in quick succession, like a machine gun.

Presentation

It is amazing how people like to fight. We see it in little children. Even an innocent toy in the hands of an expert can quickly become a lethal weapon. (Pretend to shoot the congregation with Duplo or a stick.)

But the Bible tells us that Jesus comes to bring peace. What kind of peace? There are different kinds. First there is the peace that is lovely and quiet. Parents often ask for 'a bit of peace and quiet' after Sunday dinner. I wonder if Mary and Joseph knew that kind of peace that first Christmas. (Tell the story of the stable, gradually getting softer and building a hushed atmosphere.) Then into that place Jesus comes to bring peace. (Play a tape recording of a child yelling.) I don't think it was that kind of peace!

Or there is the peace which is about understanding between nations, between countries. No wars. Everyone happy and content. Then suddenly fighting begins and shatters the peace. (Let off the poppers.) But then Jesus comes in, healing, mending, comforting. Yes, he comes to bring that kind of peace.

God is bringing peace to our world—and we are called to join in as peacemakers.

Expand on this, and give examples of contemporary Christians struggling to bring peace and justice.

Remember, 'Let there be peace on earth, and let it begin with . . . me.' God needs to start with us. (Expand and explain.)

To finish, let's close our eyes and think of someone we can't get on with and don't like. Ask God to help you to love that person and to make peace with him or her.

Mike French
Hazel Grove, Stockport

9 Ready for Christ's Return? (Keep Awake!)

Aim

To make three important points about the Second Coming of Christ and especially that we must be awake and ready for him.

Texts

Romans 13:8–14, which could be read as the Lesson; 1 Thessalonians 4:16–5:6 which should be read during the talk as indicated.

Story

The Conversion of Augustine of Hippo (Appendix 1. K).

Hymns

'Hark! a trumpet call is sounding'; 'At the name of Jesus'; 'Jesus comes with clouds descending'.

Prayers

Prayers for all the Family 6; 7; 257; 357.

Main Talk

Preparation

Prepare an OHP acetate, the top part having the words JESUS WILL RETURN AGAIN TO THIS WORLD and underneath Jesus depicted coming in glory with two angels on either side of him blowing trumpets.

On the middle to lower part have a piece of acetate to flip over, being attached by Sellotape to one side of the main acetate. On this have the words WE CANNOT KNOW WHEN and a conventional picture of a burglar, with mask and swag bag, getting into a house.

At the very bottom have a strip of acetate to flip over with the words WE MUST KEEP AWAKE AND BE READY.

Have a second acetate with a picture of someone in nightclothes, unshaven with tousled hair answering a front door.

Have a person dressed in pyjamas, dressing-gown and slippers concealed, but ready to come into church when called. Have his suit concealed near where the talk is being given.

Presentation

Ask what time of year it is in the church's calendar. Elicit the answer 'Advent' and ask what that means and whose coming we are expecting. Clearly distinguish between Jesus' first and second coming and stress that we are thinking about the second, which we say we believe in when we join in the Creed.

Proceed to make the following three main points:

(1) Jesus will return again to this world. (Show the top half of the OHP acetate.) Explain that the very early Christians, especially those living in Thessalonica, were very upset that their friends were dying and Jesus had not yet returned to the world. The Apostle Paul wrote to them about Jesus' return. Read 1 Thessalonians 4:16–17. Contrast this with Jesus' first coming.

(2) We cannot know when Jesus will return. (Flip over middle part of acetate.) Read 1 Thessalonians 5:1–4.

Explain that unfortunately burglars never give advance warning of their arrival! They may come at any time, not just at night. Though we know they may come, we are still taken by surprise. The same will be true of the Lord Jesus. Perhaps explain that a gunner in an artillery battery knows all the signs of when a gun is about to be fired, yet he still 'jumps' when it goes off.

If time allows explain that Jesus, when on earth, did not know the time of his return (Mt 24:36), so we should never take seriously anyone who attempts to tell us exactly when it is going to happen.

(3) We must keep awake and be ready. (Flip over last piece of acetate.) Read 1 Thessalonians 5:5–6. Ask if anyone thinks they have heard something similar to those verses this morning and so direct the congregation back to Romans 13:8–14.

Refer to the different clothes we wear and their significance, eg Guides and Scouts (if any are in church).

Proceed to point out that there is appropriate clothing for day and for night. At this point the person in night-clothes enters and walks up the main aisle of the church. Refer to the fact that although we were all happily wearing such clothes at 3 am this morning, most of us are not wearing these clothes now. Then point out that although we can only see one person in nightclothes, when God looks on us as a church he sees many of us wearing nightclothes. Refer to Romans 13:11–12.

Ask the person who is wearing nightclothes to attempt to put on his suit (which you bring out of hiding) on top of his nightclothes. Mention that everyone will see the impossibility and pointlessness of the exercise. But this is what most of us do spiritually. The Bible tells us to *cast off* the deeds of darkness, and having done so, to *put on* the Lord Jesus Christ and all that means.

The dramatic illustration from the life of St Augustine could come here.

'Are you ready for the return of Jesus?' Show the second acetate and refer to the passage 'The night is nearly over, the day is almost here. So let us put aside the deeds of darkness and put on the armour of light.' Will Jesus catch us still in our nightclothes?

Peter Markby
Lewes

(Note: The earlier part of this talk is based on one by Michael Botting appearing in the Scripture Union magazine *Learning All Together*, January-March 1993.)

10 The Sandwich—a Talk for Bible Sunday

AIM

To show that when we read the Bible seriously and with prayer, it nourishes us, because we feed on Jesus.

TEXT

Luke 4:16–22, which, if read as a Lesson, could be dramatised.

DRAMA

Drama for all the Family 12 'The Trip of a Lifetime' or 'O Taste and See' (Appendix 1. N).

HYMNS

Several hymn books have sections on the Scriptures. 'Father of mercies, in your word' especially highlights the teaching of this talk.

PRAYERS

The Collect appointed for Advent 2 is included in the talk. Also *Prayers for all the Family* 8; 9; 70; 155; 195; 249; 372.

MAIN TALK

Preparation

A table is needed at the front with the things necessary to make a jam sandwich.

Also you will need an old Bible (an old version from a jumble sale?) which you should cut in half down the spine so that it splits into Old and New Testaments.

A piece of card slightly bigger than the Bible, with 'Jesus' written on it.

The Collect for Advent 2 (which if not available in ASBs should be written on OHP acetate, flipchart, or printed on the notice sheet).

Presentation

Begin to make a jam sandwich and ask what is the most important part of the sandwich (the filling).

Why do we use bread? (Because it's a convenient way of holding the filling—try eating jam with your hands! Because it gives bulk to the meal—it fills us up. Because it has a goodness of its own.)

What else do we often use in a sandwich? (Butter or margarine). Why? (Because sometimes the bread is a bit dry on its own and the butter helps us digest it.)

God has given us a spiritual sandwich. The filling is Jesus. He is the centre of Christianity, for when God wanted to put the world right he sent a person.

But Jesus died 2,000 years ago—what about now? God has sent his Holy Spirit to make Jesus real to us in our daily lives.

But God has also given us another way to 'get hold' of Jesus.

It's a book in two parts (hold up the Bible and separate it into its two parts—one in each hand), rather like the two pieces of bread that make a sandwich.

Our Bible reading showed us how the two parts work.

The *New Testament* is a book about Jesus, written after his life and death and resurrection. It points us back to him.

In the Lesson (from the New Testament) Jesus read from the *Old Testament* which points forward to his coming.

But the most important part is Jesus himself who is like the filling of the sandwich (put the card with 'Jesus' written on it between the two parts of the Bible).

That's what the Bible is for—it has goodness of its own (like bread), it makes us feel full, but mainly it's supposed to help us feed on Jesus himself. Like most food it's best savoured slowly in small bites. Because it nourishes us we read it at church.

And because it is sometimes dry and difficult to digest we surround it with prayer, singing and preaching, which, like butter, helps us to digest it.

But the aim of it all is that we may feed on Jesus and know the salvation that God has brought through him.

Show the Collect for Advent 2 on OHP, pointing out the phrase about inwardly digesting, and perhaps saying it together to end.

Mark Earey
Chatham

11 Christmas with a Hole

AIM

An Advent talk designed to encourage the congregation to put Jesus back into Christmas—otherwise we have nothing to celebrate.

TEXT

Isaiah 9:2, 6–7.

DRAMA

Drama for all the Family 11 'The King is Coming'; *Acting Up* (Appendix 2), 'Nativity Scene' pp 46–48; 'No Room', pp 49–53.

STORY

Either of the two stories of Joseph (Appendix 1. L and 1.M). With some congregations *Sketches from Scripture* (Appendix 2) 'The Christmas Lecture', pp 1–5, might be appropriate.

HYMNS

See Advent section of hymn book.

PRAYERS

Prayers for all the Family 6; 257.

MAIN TALK

Preparation

You will need a small Christmas tree, fairy lights, tinsel, a fairy for the top of the tree, Christmas cards, mince pie, secular Advent calendar, Christmas *Radio/TV Times*. A Polo mint with some tinsel threaded through.

Presentation

What makes a good Christmas? Starting with the tree bring out the various things one at a time. When anyone asks 'Are you ready for Christmas?' they are not asking 'Are you ready to celebrate the wonderful birth of Jesus Christ?' They are really asking 'Have you done your mince pies and Christmas cake? Have you bought and wrapped all your presents? Have you sent your cards yet?'

That is, sadly, what Christmas is for most people—a five-day eating and drinking indulgence; a credit card spending spree; a once-a-year visit to church and a family and friends get-together. This nation of ours will be celebrating Christmas without Christ; a birthday without a birth; the coming of a kingdom without a king.

In a newspaper a few weeks before Christmas there was a full page spread advertisement. It said, 'Four things needed for a successful Christmas.' At the top was a very large turkey; below that a large Christmas pudding; below that a dish of mince pies and below that . . . a packet of indigestion tablets.

A 'successful Christmas'—it doesn't even need Christ! Or does it?

We live with people who have everything to celebrate *with*, but nothing to celebrate *about*.

Here is a small home-made decoration for the Christmas tree, a symbol of what most people's Christmas is. (Produce Polo mint.) You see—all sweetness around the outside and absolutely nothing in the middle. Nothing at the heart. (Fasten mint to tree.)

Do we as Christians also have a Polo mint Christmas? What an opportunity to witness to our faith, our joy, our thankfulness for Jesus' birth and what it means to us. Christians resolving to put Christ back into their Christmas would be the greatest and most convincing witness to their faith that there could possibly be.

Let us, when given the chance, speak out about God coming as man. Let us give time to wonder and give thanks and praise to God for his revelation of himself in Christ.

Christmas is not something thrown at us whether we like it or not. It does not come ready packaged, unchangeable, fixed. You and I can choose what is important— these trappings, or Christ. Let's resolve to put Christ into the centre of our Polo mint Christmas, so that when we gather together on Christmas Day to celebrate God born as man for our salvation we can sing the last verse of the carol in true joy and understanding of what this celebration is all about.

> Yea Lord we greet thee, Born this happy morning,
> Jesus to thee be glory given.
> Word of the Father in flesh appearing
> O come let us adore him . . .
> Christ the Lord!

Jane Parry
Crowton, Cheshire

12 What's in a Name?
A Christmas Talk

A<small>IM</small>

To explain the essential message of Christmas.

T<small>EXT</small>

Matthew 1:21.

D<small>RAMA</small>

Drama for all the Family 15 'Christmas Card'.

S<small>TORY</small>

Either of the two stories of Joseph (Appendix 1. L and 1.M).

H<small>YMNS</small>

Christmas section, especially 'Good Christian men rejoice'.

P<small>RAYERS</small>

Prayers for all the Family 12–14; 258–260.

M<small>AIN</small> T<small>ALK</small>

Preparation

Prepare two cards, one with 'Sinner' on one side and 'Your name' on the reverse side. The other card has

'Saviour' on one side and 'Jesus' on the reverse. Have either a clean blackboard with some white chalk, or an OHP acetate and non-permanent marker. Have a red cloth available.

Presentation

Ask people how many of them know the meaning of their names and produce the card with 'Your name' on it. Mention, for example, that 'George' means 'a farmer', 'Sylvia', 'a forest maiden', etc.

Most of us don't know or care about the meaning of our names, but this was not so in Bible times. 'Peter' means 'a stone'; 'Boanerges' means 'sons of thunder' and Jesus made reference to both.

However, there is a name we all have in common, a name that really describes us all. Ask for suggestions and accept the answer 'sinner'. Turn your card round. Perhaps some of us feel we have not lived very bad lives. Enlarge on the number of sins we have committed since we were born. This may be illustrated as follows.

All of us have sinned many times a day but supposing, on average, we had only sinned three times a day. Then how many sins would we have committed in a year? Go on questioning and write the following on your blackboard or OHP acetate:

For a ten-year-old: 365 x 10 x 3 = 10,950
    plus leap years, say 2   6
                               10,956 sins

For a 40-year-old   43,800
    plus leap years, say 10   30
                               43,830 sins

So sin is more serious than perhaps we thought. Elaborate on the results of sin in everyday life, such as those caused by drunken driving. But, far more serious, sin separates us from God.

Produce the other card with the name 'Jesus' showing. Ask why the Lord Jesus was given this name. Who knows what his name means? Turn to Matthew 1:21 and draw out 'Saviour' as the answer to the question, turning round the card to show 'Saviour' on the back.

Comment that Jesus lived a sinless life, otherwise he could not save sinners. He died on the cross and shed his blood for us. He rose from death to prove he is our living Saviour. His blood alone can blot out our sins. Refer to Isaiah 44:22 and 1 John 1:7.

Then wipe the blackboard or OHP acetate clean with the red cloth. End by asking whom Jesus saves and draw people's attention to 'his people'. In other words he saves those who belong to him. Ask whether everyone has given their lives to Jesus the Saviour.

Michael Botting
Editor

13 What a Difference a Baby Makes!

Aim

To compare the difference that the arrival of a couple's first baby makes with the difference which God wants to make in our lives when Jesus Christ is accepted.

Texts

Isaiah 9:6a; Luke 2:1–7; John 1:11–12.

Drama/Story

Joseph's Story 1 and 2 (Appendix 1. L and 1.M); *Ten Minute Miracle Plays* (Appendix 2) 'The Nativity', pp 79–81.

Hymns

See Christmas selection of hymn book. 'See him lying on a bed of straw', 'Sing lullaby!' and 'Thou didst leave Thy throne' would be especially suitable.

Prayers

Prayers for all the Family 12–14; 258–260.

Main Talk

Preparation

Prepare an OHP acetate with a nativity family scene of Mary, Joseph and Jesus on the top left and a modern couple holding a baby top right.

Directly underneath write 'What a difference a baby makes'. Below that write five sub-headings, which can either be directly on the acetate and gradually uncovered or can be five strips of acetate attached to either edge of the basic acetate with Sellotape, and flipped over when each point is reached.

Have a recording of a baby crying and a large doll.

Plan that there should be a couple with a real baby at church, sitting close to the worship area, so that it can be brought into church at the final moments of the talk.

Presentation

Switch on the OHP revealing the two families. Explain that as every couple knows, when the first baby comes along there are all sorts of changes we have to make to our family life, as no doubt Mary and Joseph also learned. Likewise, when we accept Jesus into our lives as our Saviour and Lord, which is why he was sent into the world, changes have to be made in our lives.

(1) There is a *new person* to consider.
Couples have somebody else to consider when they have their first child.

When we receive Jesus into our lives we have him to consider in whatever we do.

(2) There are *new priorities* in life.
Couples discover they have entirely new ideas about what things are really important.

The same is true when Jesus comes into our lives, such as the way we spend our time and money and the friends we make.

(3) There is a *new eagerness to listen*.
Play the recording of a baby crying. As soon as they hear their baby crying parents, especially mothers, dash to see if all is well. Indeed their ear is cocked to hear their baby's cry most of the time.

When we become Christians we need a similar eagerness to listen to Jesus and his call to us.

(4) There is a *new talking point*.
Most couples are always talking about their children, even if they are fed up with other people's baby talk. Grandparents can be the same with their grandchildren.

When we receive Jesus we should be willing to talk about him.

(5) There is a *new love*.
Couples often say that their new baby has brought them closer to one another.

Accepting Jesus Christ into our lives gives us a new love for God and a new love for one another.

Take the doll in one arm and have the baby brought in and placed in your other arm. Make the point that many people just want a doll of Jesus Christ, which they can pick up and play with when it suits them, and discard at other times when they are bored with him. Like new puppies or kittens or babies Jesus is for life, not just for Christmas. The offer of Christmas is a real person in Jesus Christ, but when we receive him it makes a real difference.

Peter Markby
Lewes

14 God's Communication Revolution

AIM

A Christmas talk intended to show that sending his Son was a new way of God speaking to the world, not just a nice idea.

TEXT

Hebrews 1:1–5, recommended to be read as the Lesson.

DRAMA/STORY

Christmas Hope—Joseph's Story 1 and 2 (Appendix 1. L and 1.M); *Divine Comedies*, (Appendix 2) 'Shepherd's Delight', pp 45–47; 'News of the World', pp 137–142.

HYMNS

'God has spoken—by his prophets'. See also Christmas section of the hymn book. 'A great and mighty wonder', 'Hark! the herald angels sing', 'Angels from the realms of glory', 'The first Nowell' and 'O come all you faithful' would be especially suitable.

PRAYERS

Prayers for all the Family 12–14; 258–260.

Main Talk

Preparation

If possible, have examples of different forms of communication available (megaphone, pen and paper, telephone, mobile phone, videophone, fax machine).

Have a phone set up elsewhere (hidden in the pulpit?) which will ring (or for which you can use a sound effect of ringing). You need someone who is ready to make the phone ring at the right moment.

Presentation

We are all aware of the so-called 'communications revolution'. What ways of communicating can you think of? In the old days shouting was the nearest thing to long distance communicating. Then came letter writing. (Go through all the changes, using the various objects you've managed to get to illustrate as you go.)

Christmas is about God's communications revolution.

In the past he spoke by the prophets—human beings who brought a message from God. He also used angels and sometimes dreams or visions (mention examples from the Christmas story).

But now, in Jesus, he has spoken to us by a Son—like a living, moving, breathing fax from God (but even better), who shows us what God is like and brings the message of his love. Jesus is God come in person, the very best sort of communication—face to face.

He wants to meet each of us. And that isn't just restricted to Christmas.

Have you ever been let down on a date or an appointment? God is waiting and on time. Ever felt someone was talking to you, but looking over your shoulder to someone they want to speak to next? God will give you his full attention.

But God may want to speak to us at times that are inconvenient to us, or when we least expect it (think of the angels and the dreams) and that's why we always have to be ready.

At this point the phone rings. Look flustered. Look for it. Pick it up. Without listening first you say, rather embarrassed, 'I've told you before not to ring me at work. . . . Oh! Sorry! Oh I see.' Look heavenward and edgy to give the idea that it's a call from God being put through. 'Yes of course you can reverse the charges. . . ' Listen, nod, then hold out the receiver to the congregation, saying, 'It's for you!'.

Mark Earey
Chatham

15 Christmas Trivial Pursuits

AIM

To show by means of a popular Christmas family game the facts and the importance of the incarnation.

TEXTS

Luke 2:1–7; Matthew 2:1–12.

DRAMA/STORY

Either of the two stories of Joseph (Appendix 1. L and 1.M); *Drama for all the Family* sketches 13–16.

HYMNS

Select from Christmas section of hymn book, especially hymns that name not only Jesus, but also Bethlehem and Herod.

PRAYERS

Prayers for all the Family 12–14; 258–260.

MAIN TALK

Preparation

The game 'Trivial Pursuits' wrapped up in Christmas paper.

Six cards of the following colours with words on either side:

Grey/Brown   'Art & Literature' and 'Jesus'
Yellow   'History' and 'His birth'
Blue   'Geography' and 'Bethlehem'
Pink   'Entertainment' and 'The inn'
Orange   'Sport & Leisure' and 'Herod'
Green   'Science & Nature' and 'The star'

Presentation

How good it is to receive presents at Christmas. Say that you have one which you are going to unwrap this morning. Tear off paper to reveal 'Trivial Pursuits' game. Christmas is a very good time for families and friends to play games, so we are going to play this one this morning. All the questions have something to do with the Christmas story. Explain the rules of Trivial Pursuit—how you need to answer correctly a question from each of six categories, after having landed on the appropriately coloured space on a board. We don't have a board this morning—but we do have suitably coloured cards with questions on them. Let's see if you can get the right answers!

1. Pick out the 'Art & Literature' card and ask the question: 'Who has had more books and paintings based on his life than anyone else?' When someone answers 'Jesus', get them to hold up the reverse side of the card. How amazing this is when you consider that Jesus himself never wrote a book or produced any drawings or paintings for posterity.

2. Pick out the 'History' card and ask the question: 'What event is so important that our calendars are based on it?' When someone answers 'His birth', get them to hold up

the reverse side of the card. This really is the turning point of history—divided into BC and AD.

3. Pick out the 'Geography' card and ask the question: 'In which town did the birth of Jesus take place?' When someone answers 'Bethlehem', get them to hold up the reverse side of the card. It is a real place—and people can go there today.

4. Pick out the 'Entertainment' card and ask the question: 'Where were Mary and Joseph *not* entertained?' When someone answers 'The inn', get them to hold up the reverse side of the card. This is why they finished up in the stable!

5. Pick out the 'Sport & Leisure' card and ask the question: 'Which sport-loving king did not feel very leisurely when he heard of Jesus' birth?' When someone answers 'Herod', get them to hold up the reverse side of the card. As well as building the Temple in Jerusalem, Herod also built a hippodrome where games were held—but he didn't want any rivals. Explain what happened when he heard of a new king of the Jews.

6. Pick out the 'Science & Nature' card and ask the question: 'What unusual sight was seen in the sky?' When someone answers 'The star', get them to hold up the reverse side of the card. Perhaps explain that there is evidence from elsewhere of some unusual things being seen in the sky at about the time of Jesus' birth.

You now have six people holding cards at the front. What do they mean to us?

1   Shows just how important is the Person of Jesus.

2 and 3   Show that the Christmas story is true, not a fairy story—it happened at a particular time and at a definite place.

4 and 5   Show that even then people rejected Jesus, either because they were too busy or somewhat jealous (just as today).

6   Reminds us that nothing is impossible with God—even the heavens witnessed to the coming of his Son into this world.

Jesus has changed the life of the world by actually coming into it, and he can change our lives by coming into them as well. Perhaps add that this will be no 'trivial pursuit' but a momentous event!

Peter Bannister
Taunton

16   From the Old to the New

A talk for the first Sunday of the new year designed to show some of the 'new' things which take over from the 'old' ways when we become Christians.

Text

2 Corinthians 5:17.

Drama

Drama for all the Family 31 'Home Improvements'.

Story

Christmas Story crossword from *More for all the Family* (Appendix 2) could be used, perhaps writing in from the start 16 and 21 across. 'The Bad Gang' (Appendix 1. C).

Hymns

'I do not know what lies ahead' (*Youth Praise* 102); 'Father, let us dedicate all this year to you' (*Hymns for Today's Church* 257).

PRAYERS

Prayers for all the Family 261.

MAIN TALK

Preparation

Prepare eleven cards, five or six inches high, with the following letters on them:

O L D D A I R E F W N.

At the beginning of the talk ask three children to come to the front to hold a number of cards in their hands.

The first has the letters O A R F N in that sequence, with only the O showing.

The second has the letters L D I E in that sequence, with only the L showing.

The third has the letters D W, with just the D showing.

When the Editor used this talk he also had some OHP acetates to illustrate each word. For example at the word RED he spoke about REDemption and showed blood being painted on the side posts and lintel of a Hebrew house at Passover, the cross of Jesus and a chalice of red wine.

Presentation

Explain that as we move from the old year to the beginning of the new year, it would be good to see some of the 'new' things that the Lord is wanting to show us, either as individuals or as a church. Introduce the three children, who should be holding up the letters O L D. Let's see if we can change it to the N E W by altering one letter at a time.

Remove the L from second child to display D underneath, making the word ODD. We are not meant to be 'odd' in the sense of being strange or eccentric, but we are meant to be different as Christians. Friends at school or at work should know that we are ready to stick out for what is right, even if nobody else does—like Daniel in the Old Testament.

Remove the O from the first child to display A underneath, making the word ADD. One of our aims should be for others to come to know Jesus. In Acts 2:47 it says that 'the Lord added to their group those who were being saved'. Reference could also be made to 2 Peter 1:5ff.

Remove the D from the second child to display I underneath, making the word AID. Think of people who need our help during the coming year (and groups and organisations such as Christian Aid, Band Aid, Live Aid, etc). Perhaps refer to the Good Samaritan.

Remove the A from the first child to display R underneath, making the word RID. Some things in our lives need to be thrown away! In Hebrews 12:1 (GNB) it says 'Let us rid ourselves of everything that gets in the way and of the sin which holds on to us so tightly.'

Remove the I from the second child to display E underneath, making the word RED. This always reminds us of blood, especially of the blood of Jesus, shed when he died on the cross to take away our sins and give us new life (see 1 Peter 2:24).

Remove R from the first child to display F underneath, making the word FED. If we want to grow as Christians, we need to be fed on the teaching from God's word, the Bible. (Refer to Matthew 4:4; 1 Corinthians 3:2; 1 Peter 2:2.)

Remove the D from the third child (at last!) to display W underneath, making FEW. Refer either to the gate to life being narrow, with few finding it (Mt 7:14) or to the few labourers or workers in the vineyard when there is a harvest to be reaped (Lk 10:2).

Finally, remove the F from the first child to display N underneath, making the word NEW. Link with 2 Corinthians 5:17 to show the new life which the Christian has, the old having gone. The drama could be introduced here, making the point that our lives can be compared to houses. After the sketch ask what home improvements are going to be made in the houses of our lives this new year.

Peter Bannister
Taunton

17   The Journey of Life

AIM

To show that Jesus is the Light of the world and our Guide through life.

TEXT

See Main Talk.

DRAMA

Drama for all the Family 12 'The Trip of a Lifetime'.

HYMNS

These would depend on what occasion of the year the talk was being given. 'Through all the changing scenes of life' might fit them all. Or 'I do not know what lies ahead' (*Youth Praise*, 102).

PRAYERS

These would also depend on the occasion of the presentation.

MAIN TALK

This presentation can be used for Candlemas, Christingle services, baptisms or any service on the theme of Jesus as the Light of the world, or Jesus as our guide through life. I have used it at Candlemas with Galatians 4:4–7 and Luke 2:22–40. Also for Easter 4 (Yr. 2 ASB) with 2 Corinthians 4:13–5:5 and John 14:1–11. For Candlemas I would point out that this was the day that Mary and Joseph took Jesus to the temple and that Simeon recognised the tiny baby immediately as the 'Light to lighten the Gentiles'—a light for all people.

For Easter 4 I would get the congregation to recognise that the gospel reading was from the funeral service and to link it with the New Testament reading to realise that we are all on a journey that will ultimately end in death and that however bad they may seem our troubles are really only slight and short-lived.

For a baptism I would talk about the presentation of the lit candle as the symbol of us carrying the light of Christ with us throughout our lives, whatever may be in store for us.

Preparation

Have the following life events (or make up your own) written large on A3 pieces of paper laid face downwards, and numbered on the reverse, in a trail around your church or up the central aisle starting from the chancel steps. Anglicans may want to fit in Confirmation at some point, but the popular time varies from parish to parish, so it has been omitted from the following lists.

1. Birth and baptism
2. Birth of sister
3. Starts school
4. Gets bullied
5. Starts secondary school
6. Girlfriend trouble and fails some exams
7. Starts college
8. Gets a job
9. Love and marriage
10. Father dies
11. Birth of a child
12. Loses job
13. Marriage under strain
14. Another child born
15. Gets another job

16. Marriage improves
17. Promotion and moves house
18. Eldest child involved with drugs
19. Marriage under strain
20. Made redundant
21. Moves to a smaller house
22. Wife retrains and gets a job
23. Mother dies
24. Children leave home
25. Retires
26. Wife dies
27. Residential home
28. Death

Presentation

Some people have a real problem with thinking of a candle as a symbol of Christ because it is so fragile and vulnerable and so easily extinguished. Others have a problem with the concept of walking in the light because so often it feels as if we are in the dark. It all made sense to me when I saw a picture on the TV news of a Bosnian family who were crouched in their cellar clutching a candle, having been without electricity for two years.

Two things suddenly struck me. One is that if you are using a candle for light you have to make a conscious effort to carry it around with you and you can't ignore it once it is on like an electric light. The other is that if it is really dark and you are relying on a candle you can't actually see very far in front of you. You can only see enough to take one step at a time. In other words you need an element of faith to trust Jesus to guide you on your journey. In life we cannot see the future or where we are going but with faith in Christ we can see enough to take the next step.

We are going to take a journey through the life of Joe Bloggs.

Recruit a Joe Bloggs and his parents. Give Joe an unlit candle in a holder and explain that you are going to take him on a journey through his life. Lead him and his parents to life event number one which he picks up and shows to the congregation. Light the candle to signify his baptism. Take him on through his life step by step, recruiting extra people as needed, eg sister, wife, children and losing them as they die. Tell the story of his life as you go along, talking about the nature of the ups and downs and the points where his faith might waver and his candle nearly go out, and where he summons up the faith to go on. When Joe reaches his death, blow out the candle and ask someone why he doesn't need the candle any more.

Conclude by saying that it is probably a good thing that we cannot see what life holds for us because if we did we might not ever begin, but that as Christians we do believe that God is with us and that we carry the candle of Jesus' love to guide and strengthen us through whatever lies ahead of us.

Rosemary Miller
Grantham

18 Education Sunday (Ninth Sunday before Easter)

AIM

To show that what we do in our lives and with our lives will have to be accounted for to God.

TEXT

Matthew 25:14–30, which should certainly be read as the Lesson and could be dramatised, using the version in *The Dramatised Bible*, p 57 New Testament section.

HYMNS

'Teach me, my God and King'. See also suggestions in *Hymns for Today's Church* under 9th Sunday before Easter: Christ the Teacher.

PRAYERS

Prayers for all the Family 159; 226.

MAIN TALK

Preparation

Acquire from four or five members of the congregation of various ages one of their school reports. Also, if possible, acquire for yourself a gown, mortar board and cane.

On an OHP acetate write up God's report as shown below.

Presentation

'Good morning, class!' (This should elicit the response of a 'Good morning' in return. Repeat the greeting severely if not, and it will be returned!)

'We have come to that time of year when the school reports are read out, and, oh dear—we do have some backsliders, don't we?'

Read out some of the comments on the reports and get the congregation to guess whose report it is. School reports try to pass on information about how you are doing in your subject: whether you are making an effort at your work, what kind of person you are—helpful or disruptive, keen or lazy. The little comments next to each subject are meant to be encouraging—'works well'; 'pleasing results'; 'excellent progress'.

Then there are the comments of 'needs to pay attention'; 'not doing as well as could be expected'; 'must try harder'. These remarks are intended to spur on to improvement and a more wholehearted approach to the work. Teachers don't expect pupils to be perfect in all their subjects but they want their pupils to try and do the very best that they can.

God doesn't expect us to be perfect in our Christian lives, but he wants us to try our very best.

If God was to give us his school report on our Christianity, what comments, encouragements and criticism would he make?

It is often said that we learn more when we leave school than we ever did when we were there; we just keep on learning through life. The same is true of being a Christian. There isn't a point at which we stop—'I'm a Christian now and that's it.' Every day we learn more of what

SUBJECT	GOD'S COMMENT
Kindness to others	Improving, but must remember that kindness must also extend to people you don't really like or who don't like you.
Giving of money to God's house and God's work	Has a tendency to deep pockets and short arms.
Prayer and worship	Enthusiastic when roused. I would rather talk with this pupil on a daily basis than just on a Sunday morning. Bible study and revision sadly lacking.

being a Christian really means—through prayer, through Bible reading, through people we meet, things we see and read. Growing up and learning as a Christian never stop.

There are many aspects of our Christian lives where we know only too well that we are backsliding and need greater effort. God knows it too!

Prayer life non-existent? Just get talking to God and tell him everything that is happening in your world. Find a book of prayers that help you say to God what you want. If you were studying for an English A-level and your subject was Arthur Miller, then you would be encouraged to read many of his books to get to know this author. Read the Gospels. Jesus said, 'Anyone who has seen me has seen the Father.' Get to know what Jesus shows us of God.

People who study hard and make obvious efforts often get labelled 'swots' and that label can be hard to live with. Should your efforts be noticed by your parents, friends or children you may likewise be ridiculed. But like those studying for exams you must hold on to your goal—a deepening relationship and understanding of God our Father. Who knows what small seed you may have planted in being discovered to be learning about him?

Then through his grace, when God gives us each our final 'school report', he will say to us too, 'Well done, good and faithful servant.'

Class dismissed!

Jane Parry
Crowton, Cheshire

19 Jesus' Temptations—a Talk for Lent

To show how Jesus was tempted by Satan in the desert, and how eventually he won the victory, just as we can when we trust in him.

TEXT

Matthew 4:1–11 which can be read dramatically using a narrator, Satan and Jesus. See *The Dramatised Bible*, p 5 in the New Testament section.

DRAMA

Drama for all the Family 36 'Lead Us Not Into. . . '; *Scenes and Wonders* 'The Alternative Ten Commandments' pp 64ff; 'Guilty Conscience' (Appendix 1.P), *Ten Minute Miracle Plays* (Appendix 2) 'The Temptation of Jesus', pp 124–127.

STORY

Read a passage from *The Screwtape Letters* by C.S. Lewis (eg Chapter 2).

HYMNS

Lent section of hymn book, especially the hymns 'Forty days and forty nights'; 'Father God in heaven' (a metrical version of the Lord's Prayer); 'Lead us, heavenly Father, lead us'.

PRAYERS

Prayers for all the Family 7; 30; 203; 217; 370–375; 407.

MAIN TALK

Preparation

Prepare five acetate sheets that overlap, so that eventually they form a cross which also takes the form of a sword or dagger striking into Satan.

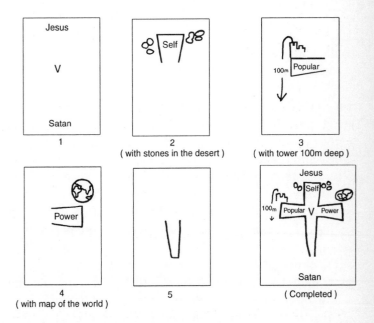

Presentation

Tell people that you want to try out a little experiment. Whatever they do in the next few minutes, they must *avoid* thinking about white elephants, or how their favourite football team is getting on, or about what they are going to have for dinner. Now, hands up anyone who immediately began to think of any of those things as soon as I said them!

It's like that with temptation. It's not wrong to be tempted—it's only wrong to give way to it. We know this because Jesus himself was tempted. In fact this was the biggest battle of all time.

OHP 1. Jesus v Satan

Jesus had just been baptised, and then he went out into the desert, where he was hungry and alone. It was then that Satan came along to tempt him. Explain that Satan (the devil) isn't some kind of comic figure with a three-pronged fork, but someone who will try to get us to do things that are wrong. Very often he will come along when everything is going very well or it may be when we are facing big problems. Look how he tempted Jesus.

OHP 2. Self

Jesus was feeling hungry, so Satan tried to get him to use his powers to turn the stones in the desert into bread—simply to satisfy his own need. The temptation was along the lines of 'Me first', 'I want'. But Jesus would not do this.

OHP 3. Popularity

Satan then tried to get Jesus to throw himself off the highest point of the Temple into the valley below (about 450 feet or 100 metres) and get the angels to save him. Think of how popular he would be then, when people saw what had happened! But Jesus would never perform miracles to get people to follow him.

OHP 4. Power

Have you ever thought of what you would do if you were the ruler of the world? That was the next way in which Satan tempted Jesus—to be given all this power if only Jesus would worship him. In fact, Satan conveniently overlooked the fact that the world really does belong to Jesus. But Jesus had come into the world in a very humble way, and never looked for power for its own sake. And he would certainly not worship Satan.

Each time Jesus answered Satan by telling him what was the true message of the Bible. This is the best thing to do when we are tempted. We are told that Satan left Jesus. But he would be back.

Jesus felt the full impact of temptation three years later, when Satan tried to get him to avoid the cross.

OHP 5

When Jesus died on the cross, it must have seemed that Satan had won. However, Jesus was to rise again, and Satan's days since then have been numbered. The cross is like a dagger striking a death-blow at Satan. He still fights a very fierce rearguard action, though, and will continue to tempt us. But the victory belongs to Jesus, and the Bible tells us that 'because he himself suffered when he was tempted, he is able to help those who are being tempted' (Heb 2:18).

Peter Bannister
Taunton

20 Mothering Sunday (1) Christian Holiness

To recognise that many of the traditional motherly virtues are part of Christian holiness to which all Christians should aspire.

TEXT

Colossians 3:12–14.

DRAMA

Drama for all the Family 31 'Home Improvements'; *Divine Comedies* (Appendix 2) 'Smothers Day', pp 160–164.

STORY

In 1878 when William Booth's Salvation Army had just been so named, men from all over the world began to enlist. One man, who had once dreamed of himself as a bishop, crossed the Atlantic from America to England to enlist. He was a Methodist minister called Samuel Logan Brengle. And he now turned from a fine pastorate to join Booth's Salvation Army. Brengle later became the Army's first American-born Commissioner.

At first Booth accepted Brengle's services reluctantly and grudgingly. Booth said to him, 'You've been your own boss too long.' And in order to instil humility into Brengle, he set him to work cleaning the boots of the other trainees.

Brengle said to himself, 'Have I followed my dream across the Atlantic in order to black boots?'

Then, as in a vision, he saw Jesus bending over the feet of rough, unlettered fishermen.

'Lord,' he whispered, 'you washed their feet; I will black their boots.' (*The General Next to God* by Richard Collier (Collins: Glasgow, 1965).

HYMNS

'Amazing grace!'; 'For the beauty of the earth'; 'Happy the home that welcomes you, Lord Jesus'; 'I'm accepted'; 'Jesus, good above all others'.

PRAYERS

Prayers for all the Family 34; 87; 117; 244.

MAIN TALK

Preparation

Write Colossians 3:12 on an OHP acetate.

The job description for a mum (see below) might also go onto an acetate.

Obtain the following articles of clothing: St John's Ambulance beret, a chef's hat, some rubber gloves, a sports coach's hat, a watch.

Presentation

On this Mothering Sunday, if you and I were writing a job description for a desirable mum, what are some of the qualities we should look for?

– a good cook
– an efficient, but invisible cleaner
– an instantly available chauffeur
– a walking encyclopaedia
– a trouble-shooter to clear up little accidents which happen
– a non-interfering shoulder to cry on.

Quite a list! Is it any wonder that mums often feel pretty daunted?

Let's try a different description and it's such an important one that we're going to learn it. Show acetate of Colossians 3:12.

Who's this describing? A mum? After all, those qualities all sound rather like the ideal qualities of a mum.

Actually, no. That description is one that applies to all Christian people. It's St Paul's description of Christians. (Repeat the text again.)

There are two important parts in this Bible verse—the first part's about who you and I are. The second is about what we can do. Listen carefully to the verse: 'As God's *chosen* people, holy and dearly loved. . . ' You and I are *chosen*!

Ask if anyone's been chosen to play in a sporting event. Enlarge on the thrill of it. When it comes to being selected for God's team things are different. It is not based on past achievement, but simply because you're *you*, and you're special, precious to God and chosen to be in his team— God's global team! (Repeat the first half of the text.)

Now comes the second part of the verse: 'Clothe yourselves with compassion, kindness, humility, gentleness and patience.'

When I was chosen to represent my school, it made me very determined to win. I was dead keen to do my best for

the teacher who'd selected me. That was my motivation—
I wanted to please my teacher.

The motivation for being a Christian should be similar. I
want to do my best in order to please God, who amazingly,
and without my deserving it, has chosen me to be in his
team.

So what does this mean? What does God want of us?
(Refer back to text.)

I have here some clothes to help us understand this, but
I need five volunteers.

1. Compassion (beret). Talk about the compassion
shown by members of the St John's Ambulance who are
always on duty at all sorts of public events. Stress that
compassion is not just sitting in front of the TV and being
sorry for people in trouble, but actually doing something
about it to help them.

2. Kindness (chef's hat). Talk about making a delicious
cake for someone just to show you care. God wants us to
think about ways in which we can be kind to people to
show we care. Give or ask for examples.

3. Humility (rubber gloves). Talk about swallowing
pride and being prepared to do the grotty jobs (see the
Story above). Give or ask for examples.

4. Gentleness (coach's hat). Talk about how a team
coach has to be an encourager, spurring people on to do
their best. Someone who gently pushes other people and
isn't out for personal gain. Ask if people are good at
encouraging their friends, rather than criticising them.

5. Patience (watch). Patience is all about waiting while
others catch up. It's about including other people, even if
they aren't necessarily very good at something. It's about
giving up time, when you could be doing other things, to
spend with someone who needs you. Give or ask for
examples.

Recap your main points, linking them to the text, and dismiss the team of helpers.

On this Mothering Sunday, as we show our appreciation for our mothers, let all of us ask God's help to become increasingly like the people he wants us to be: compassionate, kind, humble, gentle and patient.

Peter Chantry
Joint Youth Officer,
Diocese of Chester

21 Mothering Sunday (2)
Mothers and the Church

AIM

To show that Jesus Christ is sufficient for our spiritual needs.

TEXT

Colossians 1:13–14; 3:12–16.

DRAMA

Drama for all the Family 17 'Happy Families'. This drama is chosen to draw attention to the fact that nowadays the emphasis on Mothering Sunday should be on all the family, not just mothers.

HYMNS

'For the beauty of the earth'; 'Happy the home that welcomes you, Lord Jesus'; 'Jesus, good above all others'.

PRAYERS

Prayers for all the Family 34; 87; 117; 244.

MAIN TALK

Preparation

In advance of the service you need to recruit four helpers, who will require the following equipment:

(a) First-aid box, crepe bandage, nurse's cap, large medicine bottle.
(b) Apron, kitchen tools, tin opener, saucepan, shopping basket.
(c) Hot water bottle, cushion, vase of (plastic) flowers.
(d) Dustpan and brush, bucket and cloth, box of soap flakes.

Large labels should be made to hang round the necks of the helpers, marked: Healing, Feeding, Comforting, Washing.

Presentation

Today is Mothering Sunday, when we especially think of our human mothers, but also of 'mother' church, and the whole church family.

Draw attention to the fact that mothers deal with many different matters:

1. Healing

Hand a label to the first helper and dress with props mentioned in (a) above. Remind the congregation that mothers give first aid, say when a knee is cut, there's something in your eye or a pain in your tummy.

Ask how 'mother' church brings Jesus' healing. Elicit answers such as through prayer, the laying on of hands, sometimes through anointing with oil, and through the love of other church members (Col 3:12–14).

2. Feeding

Hand a label and dress with the props mentioned in (b) above. Our mothers are concerned to provide us with a healthy diet of food through their shopping and cooking.

Ask what food 'mother' church provides. Elicit the food and drink of God's word (Col 3:16. See also 1 Corinthians 3:1–2; Hebrews 5:12–14; 1 Peter 2:2). Also worship and fellowship.

3. Comforting

Hand the label and dress with props listed in (c). Mothers turn houses into homes with carpets and curtains, cushions and proper bed-making.

Ask how 'mother' church provides for our comfort. Elicit the comfort and strength of the Holy Spirit, the peace of Christ and the assurance of God's everlasting arms (Col 3:15).

4. Washing

Hand the label and dress with props listed in (d) above. Mention the time that mothers spend in keeping our homes clean and tidy. Ask how 'mother' church makes us clean. Refer to Colossians 1:13–14 and 3:14.

Mention that human mothers may get very tired or be ill, but not the Lord (Is 40:28–31). We mustn't take mothers for granted or take for granted the power, nourishment and forgiveness of Christ by ignoring it ungratefully.

Ken Jamieson
Taunton

22 Palm Sunday—a Day of Contradictions

To show that Jesus is King and must become King of all aspects of our lives.

Zechariah 9:9 and Matthew 21:1–11.

Drama for all the Family 58 'The Dishonest Steward'.

See Palm Sunday section in church hymn book. Also suitable are Graham Kendrick's 'Make Way'; 'Rejoice! Rejoice! Christ is in you', and Mary Smail's 'Prepare the way of the Lord' in *Songs of Fellowship* (Kingsway).

Prayers for all the Family 37; 263; 380; 381.

Preparation

Prepare the following OHP acetates as illustrated:

1. Jesus apparently about to throw himself from the pinnacle of the Temple.
2. A blank acetate with three acetates attached
   (a) Jesus on a donkey in the centre
   (b) A crowd on left and right with space for Jesus
   (c) Jesus on a horse in the centre
3. Is Jesus King of our . . .
   Moments? with a clock opposite
   Mind? with a furrowed brow
   Money? with an investment bureau, cashier and piggy-bank.
These should be able to be flipped over.

Presentation

Ask what a contradiction is. Explain that on the first Palm Sunday Jesus twice behaved in the opposite way to what might have been expected.

1. Forcing choice. (OHP of Jesus on pinnacle of the Temple.) At the beginning of his public ministry Jesus was tempted to throw himself down and be unharmed, so that everyone would follow him. But he refused.

During the ministry that followed he performed miracles of healing, but he always told people to keep it quiet. He fed the Five Thousand, but then hid himself.

Now he comes out in public display and fulfils the prophecy of Zechariah 9:9. (Read.) (OHP of crowd with Jesus on donkey.) He declares himself King and everyone has to make up their minds.

We are constantly having to make decisions: which TV programme to watch, what clothes to buy, which food to choose, which crowd to follow, which party to vote for. We cannot sit on the fence for ever.

For three years people could make up their minds about Jesus, but now he forces them to do so, choosing a donkey of peace, not a horse of war; by cleansing the Temple; by very direct teaching. The religious leaders got the message and decided to have him killed.

Have you made up your mind about him? (Read 2 Corinthians 6:2.)

Three devils were discussing how they could keep humans from following Jesus. One said, 'Tell them there's no heaven.' Another said, 'Tell them there's no hell.' But the one who got Satan's prize was the one who said, 'Tell them there's no hurry.'

2. Peaceful strength.

We usually admire the strong man. Our heroes are powerful. Give examples. The Jews thought that Jesus was going to help them to be victorious over the Romans who ruled Israel/Palestine. They thought he should come into Jerusalem on a horse (OHP change donkey for horse).

Zechariah spoke of war horses, but Jesus chose the gentle, peaceful donkey.

The world chooses armed force—the bomb and the bullet. The great powers of Rome, France, Nazi Germany, etc, have chosen armed force and lost. The peaceful army of Jesus still marches. (Possibly read from Romans 12:12–21; 2 Corinthians 10:3–4.)

3. Is Jesus our King? (OHP)

Comment briefly on Christ's kingship of our Moments, Mind and Money.

Michael Botting
Editor

THROW YOURSELF DOWN
TELL NO ONE
HE HID HIMSELF

IS JESUS KING OF OUR...

MOMENTS ?

MIND ?

MONEY ?

23   The Triumph of the Cross

AIM

To show how the cross of Jesus has brought real freedom.

TEXT

Colossians 2:8–15.

DRAMA

Drama for all the Family 32 'The Right Credentials'.

STORY

A young Spanish boy prided himself on the quality of the chains he made. Each link was actually embossed with his special mark. Anyone would recognise his chains. But the young man had a fiery temper which one day landed him in trouble and eventually into prison.

Because he made several attempts to escape, the authorities had to resort to chaining him to the wall of his cell. To the prisoner's horror, as he examined his chains, he discovered every link had a mark that he knew only too well. He was securely held prisoner by the work of his own hands—in more than one sense!

HYMNS

Any appointed for Passiontide, like 'There is a green hill'. Wesley's hymn 'And can it be' is also suitable (see especially verse 4).

PRAYERS

Prayers for all the Family 4; 264–270.

MAIN TALK

Preparation

Put the following words in large letters on cardboard with suitable material to fix around volunteer captives as indicated:

1. *Consequences*—with chains and a padlock
2. *Habits*—with ropes and a padlock
3. *Fears*—with chains or ropes and a padlock.

Have three keys, none of which will open the padlocks, with labels on them marked 'good works', 'Christian home', 'church attendance'. Have the three keys that *do* unlock the padlocks all attached to a cardboard cross, say about 9" tall.

Prepare the following acetates for the OHP:

1. Colossians 2:8 written out with the word 'captive' emphasised. The following strips should be able to be flipped over at the appropriate moment:

(a) Chained by consequences of the past
(b) Held by habits of the present
(c) Fettered by fears of the future

2. The word 'freedom' on another acetate with the following strips:

(a) Fullness (small picture of a manger, cross and empty tomb)

  (b) Fellowship (picture of cross and baptism)
  (c) Forgiveness (cross and a note that can be added, as if nailed to the cross)
  (d) The cross
  (e) The Holy Spirit
  (f) Heaven

Presentation

Refer to any famous or notorious people being held captive these days, but then stress that we are all captives. However the good news of the cross (or Good Friday, if the talk is being given on that day) is that we need be captives no longer.

1. Captives

Ask for your volunteer captive and explain with suitable illustrations that we are all chained by the consequences of our past life, perhaps telling the story mentioned above. Put the chain round your captive, fixing the padlock and switching on the OHP to show the text and 'Chained by consequences of the past'.

  Proceed in a similar way with Habits, mentioning drugs as being an extreme illustration.

  Then proceed with Fears, say of unemployment, illness, death, etc, pointing out that Jesus taught that worry was a kind of sin.

  Explain that the message of Paul to the Colossians was that the world offers various solutions, but that they all lead *into* captivity, not out of it. Only in Jesus can we find real freedom. Read verse 8. How does this come about? The next verses explain.

2. Freedom (OHP)

(a) Fullness (OHP) (Verse 9.) Jesus is God in human form, which is why his unique birth and genuine physical resurrection are so important and vital to what we believe.

If the recommended drama has been used, refer to the fact that the man thought his good deeds were the right credentials for getting to heaven. The only one to have the right credentials was Jesus for he alone was sinless and therefore fully free.

(Verse 10.) In him is all the power we need to escape fully from our chains.

(b) Fellowship (OHP) (Verses 11–12.) The way Jesus made it possible for us to receive our freedom was not by putting off a little bit of flesh, as in circumcision, but by giving his whole life in dying for us on the cross on that first Good Friday. Explain that we make it *our* freedom by repentance and faith, illustrated by baptism. In that way we enter into a close personal fellowship with Christ.

(c) Forgiveness (OHP) (Verses 13–15.) If we are genuinely sorry for our sins we could write them down and imagine them nailed to the cross, where Jesus deals with them. (OHP—add note to cross.)

Conclusion
Return to your 'captive'. Attempt to use the 'worldly' keys, which prove ineffective. Then use 'cross' keys. When 'Consequences' comes off, put 'The cross' on the OHP and explain that it is on the cross that Jesus has dealt with the penalty of the past. When 'Habits' comes off explain that it is in the power of the Holy Spirit (OHP) that we are enabled to overcome these. When 'Fears' comes off refer to the fact that through the cross Jesus was able to unlock the gate of heaven (OHP) and let us in. As Christians we need not fear the future, for whatever the immediate problems, ultimately there is heaven itself.

Possibly end by referring to the time when Paul appeared before Agrippa in Acts 26, physically chained, but really the only free man present. And/or tell the story of the Frenchman who became a naturalised Englishman. 'Previously,' he said, 'I had lost the Battle of Waterloo, now I have won it!' Apply this to our joining Jesus' victory side.

Michael Botting
Editor

24 The Big Draw

AIM

To show that when Jesus Christ is lifted up before people, he will draw them to himself as he promised.

TEXT

John 12:32.

DRAMA

Drama for all the Family 18 'The Passion'.

STORY

The crucifixion narrative from one of the Gospels.

HYMNS

'When Christ was lifted from the earth' (*Hymns for Today's Church* 335). See Passion section of hymn book.

PRAYERS

Prayers for all the Family 264–270 based on the Words from the Cross.

MAIN TALK

Preparation

Prepare a series of large pictures on the life of Jesus from birth to Whitsuntide, each picture bearing a letter of the words BIG DRAW, as illustrated. You will need to have some means of suspending them, the top being fairly high, so that subsequent ones can come under it in order.

Alternatively everyone in the congregation could be provided with a leaflet with the pictures.

Presentation

Lots of people waste their money on gambling these days, probably more so now that the National Lottery has been introduced. If we live by trust in God, we shall never need to turn to such ways of making money.

Our Father God sent his Son from the riches of heaven into this world to be our Saviour and, when he was here, he gave to mankind what gambling people would call the 'BIG DRAW'. What do we mean? Well, one day he said, 'When I am lifted up from the earth, I will draw all men to myself.' He was referring to the way in which he was to die in order to save us from our sins. He would be lifted up on the cross and this would attract people to him.

However his whole life is one 'BIG DRAW' when you look at it. Jesus was such a magnetic personality, drawing people of all kinds to consider his life story and respond to it.

Proceed to speak very briefly about what the 'BIG DRAW' stands for, adding each picture in turn as you do so, or referring to the leaflet.

BIRTH

IDENTITY

GOSPEL

DEATH

RESURRECTION

ASCENSION

WHITSUNTIDE

Birth
Identity (who was he?)
Gospel (he was and is Good News!)

Death
Resurrection
Ascension
Whitsun (when God the Holy Spirit came to carry on
  the work)

Go on to explain that Jesus gives us:
  Birth to a new life
  Inspiration for life
  Good News about life

  Dignity in life
  Resurrection life
  Action for life
  Witness to his life

Let him draw you and use you to draw others to him.

Bill Woods
Wolverhampton

25   Easter Eggs

AIM

To retell the Easter story for young children.

TEXT

John 20:16 (AV).

DRAMA

Scenes and Wonders (Appendix 2) 'Easter Eggs and Easter Errors'.

STORY

Henrietta the Hen (Appendix 1. Q).

HYMNS

See Easter section from church hymn book.

PRAYERS

Prayers for all the Family 41; 271; ASB 1980 pp 573–4, Collects appointed for Easter Day.

Main Talk

Preparation

Cut out six cards in different colours in the shape of large eggs, with E on one card, A on the next and so on, to spell the word 'EASTER'. On the back of the first 'E', print an 'M' in the same size as the other letters.

Presentation

Ask the children who had Easter eggs today. Ask for five volunteers to hold cards. Then draw out from the children the Easter story. Who first came to find Jesus? What time of the day was it? Elicit the word 'early' and produce the first E which you hold up yourself.

Where was Jesus' body buried? Draw out the word 'tomb' and produce the T of Easter and hand it to a child to hold up.

Who did the tomb belong to? Draw out the words 'Joseph of Arimathaea' and produce the A, which you hand to another child to hold up.

What was in front of the tomb? Draw out the words 'stone, soldiers and seal', and put the S in front of the T.

What did the ladies find when they got to the tomb? Draw out the word 'empty' and perhaps make reference to the 'earthquake' and put the next E up.

What was the message of the angel? That Jesus was risen. Produce the R.

Talk about Mary of Magdala, who remained in the garden weeping, mentioning how the Lord Jesus had said her many sins were forgiven. Jesus had brought her a new life, but now she thought he was dead and everything was over. Suddenly she saw the gardener and asked him where Jesus had been laid. Upon discovering that the gardener was after all Jesus, ask the children what Mary called him. If the AV has been read you should be able to draw out the answer 'Master'. Turn round the first E of EASTER to reveal the M—so spelling 'MASTER'. Ask the congregation whether Jesus is their Master too.

Michael Botting
Editor

26 The Wrong End of the Stick

AIM

To show how the news of the resurrection turns things upside down, bringing triumph out of seeming tragedy.

TEXT

John 20:1–10.

DRAMA

Drama for all the Family 22 'Sherlock Holmes Investigates . . . The Case of the Missing Corpse'; *Acting Up* (Appendix 2) 'Easter Morning', pp 93–94.

STORY

After the Battle of Waterloo the English look-outs waited for news of the struggle. Through the mist they saw the signals. 'Wellington,' the message read, 'defeated . . .' and then the mists closed in. They were disappointed and sad.

However the next day as they looked again the full message came through: 'Wellington defeated . . .' as before, but now two more words: '. . . the French.' Defeat was now victory. Sadness was turned to joy. They had originally got 'the wrong end of the stick'.

HYMNS

See Easter section of hymn book.

PRAYERS

Prayers for all the Family 41; 271; ASB 1980 pp 573–4, Collects appointed for Easter Day.

MAIN TALK

Preparation

Obtain a stick long enough to take seven cards loosely drawing-pinned to it with letters on them: E V I L W O N. The cards should be able to swivel round easily through 180 degrees.

Presentation

Have you ever got hold of the wrong end of the stick? Give one or two personal examples. Then tell story above.

After the crucifixion of Jesus the disciples were understandably dispirited and dejected. They thought evil had won. Show visual aid with EVIL WON.

All seemed gloom and despair. However on Easter Sunday, as the mists rose, the full and correct message became apparent. News came that the tomb was empty, that Jesus was risen. On Good Friday the disciples had misunderstood. They had got the wrong end of the stick.

Turn the stick over so that the letters swing through 180

degrees revealing N O W L I V E. Sadness was changed to joy. Defeat had become victory. The message of death was now the offer of life, starting now and going on for ever.

At times we can get hold of the wrong end of the stick, but God's hand is in control, changing apparent defeat into triumph.

Eric Leese
Nuneaton

27   Easter Means New Life

AIM

To demonstrate that the empty tomb meant new life for Jesus and can mean new life for us too.

TEXTS

John 20:1–2; 11–16; 19–20; 24–29.

DRAMA

Drama for all the Family 21 'Jesus is back' or 22 'Sherlock Holmes Investigates . . . The Case of the Missing Corpse'; *Acting Up* (Appendix 2), 'Easter Morning', pp 93–94.

STORY

'Henrietta the Hen' (Appendix 1. Q).

HYMNS

See Easter section of hymn book.

PRAYERS

Prayers for all the Family 41; 271; ASB 1980 pp 573–4, Collects appointed for Easter Day.

MAIN TALK

Preparation

Have ready some chocolate Easter eggs and some sweet 'pigeons' eggs'. Also a tray with several hardboiled eggs in egg cups plus one empty shell turned upside down in its egg cup.

If possible prepare some OHP pictures to illustrate (a) a churchyard, (b) a tomb in a hillside and (c) several sealed tombs with one where the stone is rolled away.

Presentation

Boiled eggs for breakfast . . . have you played the pretend game of 'have another' at breakfast time? When you've finished your egg, secretly turn it upside down and pretend to give it to someone else as another egg for them to eat.

Can anyone guess which is the 'pretend' one on this tray? They all look the same on the outside . . . but the empty one is different.

If you found an empty shell in a bird's nest, what would it show? You'd know a baby bird had been born from it. The *empty* shell means *new life*.

We have eggs at Easter as a symbol to remind us of *new life*.

When people die in this country we often bury them in a churchyard. When Jesus died in Palestine people were buried in tombs, holes cut in the rocky hillside.

There were probably lots of tombs in Jerusalem. How could you tell which one was Jesus' tomb?

The *empty* one is different . . . it means *new life*.

How do we know Jesus is really alive?

1. It's a historical fact that the tomb was empty.
2. Witnesses tell us they saw Jesus after that:
   Mary recognised Jesus' voice.

Thomas recognised Jesus' wounds.

The disciples met Jesus.

But is that enough?

Show your dish of pigeons' eggs sweets. If I told you these pigeon's eggs were really sweets, would you believe me? There's only one way to find out . . . anyone want to test them for themselves?

We may believe what other people tell us, but if we want to be sure it's true *we have to taste and see for ourselves*.

Sheila Lloyd
Braintree

28 Jesus the Pioneer—a Talk for Ascensiontide

A<small>IM</small>

To teach that Jesus has pioneered the road to heaven for us to accept and follow.

T<small>EXT</small>

John 14:6.

D<small>RAMA</small>

Drama for all the Family 26 'Climbing'.

S<small>TORY</small>

'Mo's Fall' (Appendix 1.D).

H<small>YMNS</small>

See Ascensiontide section of hymn book.

P<small>RAYERS</small>

Prayers for all the Family 48–50; 215; 256; 272; 393.

MAIN TALK

Preparation

Ideally have someone all dressed up in climbing gear. Alternatively have a climbing rope and a large picture or OHP acetate of a mountaineer rock-climbing.

The talk has been put into the third person, but if you have been rock-climbing, like the author, then it will be that much more telling if put into the first person.

Presentation

Ask if anyone has ever been a Scout, Guide or Sea Cadet. One of the things you would most certainly have been taught would be how to tie knots. One of the most important is the bowline. Show how to tie it, either on yourself or on your volunteer climber (having previously checked that you can!). Possibly ask one of the Scouts etc, in the congregation to do it.

Enquire why the bowline is so important, and elicit the answer that the knot cannot slip. Show picture of a mountaineer rock-climbing, with the rope round his middle and the other end securely tied at the top of the climb. Of course rock-climbers are dependent on someone else going ahead first and taking the rope with him. What do we call a person who goes somewhere or does something first? Elicit the answer 'a pioneer'.

People often think of life like that. Not perhaps so much a climb as a *journey*. They think of life as a journey not to old age, wearing out and death, but to heaven and a wonderful new life with God. Jesus obviously saw life in that way. In his famous Sermon on the Mount he said, 'Small is the gate and narrow *the road* that leads to life, and only a few find it' (Mt 7:14). Then towards the end of his life on earth, when he was preparing his disciples for his departure, he told them they should not be sad for he was going to prepare a place for them. He then assured them, 'I am the way and the truth and the life. No-one comes to the Father except through me' (Jn 14:6).

If we are Christians, that means we have accepted that way for ourselves. We can say we came from God; we belong to God; we are going to God. So life is a journey leading eventually to heaven. We may well have troubles and difficulties on the way, but we know that Jesus has gone before us. He has pioneered the way, and he has left us the rope. We must hold on to the rope, and follow Jesus' way, and we will reach the end of our journey.

There is a special reason for thinking about all this today. Does anyone know why? Elicit the answer 'Ascension Day'. That is the day when we remember and celebrate Jesus reaching the end of his very special journey. He had died on the cross on Good Friday and been raised from the grave on Easter Day. He pioneered the way for us to follow, and left us with the rope. We must grab it, hold onto it, and follow with fresh courage and assurance.

We come from God; we belong to God; we are going to God—firmly holding Jesus' rope, and firmly fixed to it.

Michael Grylls
Whitchurch, Hants

29 The Coming of the Holy Spirit at Pentecost

Aᵢₘ

AIM

To show that the Holy Spirit changes and enables us.

TEXT

Acts 2:1–4, 36.

PRAYERS

Prayers for all the Family 51; 52; 200; 395.

DRAMA/STORY/HYMNS

All included in the outline below.

Preparation

A group of children should rehearse the following mime, to be performed during the reading. Get the children to sit on chairs draped with sheets, and to act that they are the frightened disciples. Use a Hoover to make the sound of wind. Adults hidden behind the chairs should produce 'flames' on coloured card, or crepe paper streamers on sticks. The children then get up and go off saying, 'Jesus, Jesus is Lord!'

Two or three people should be asked to prepare short and to-the-point testimonies, one of God giving words and courage to speak of Jesus; one of God enabling the person to care for others; and one of God enabling the person to worship.

Write up on an OHP a simple chorus in a foreign language, eg 'Yes, Jesus loves me', either in French:

> *Oui, Jèsus m'aime*, (×3)
> *La Bible me l'a dit.*

Or in Persian:

> *Bale, doost dah-rad* (×3)
> *Ketah-bash meegooyad.*

Presentation

Song: 'When the Spirit of the Lord is within my heart'.

Confession: The fruit of the Spirit is love, joy and peace. Father, we confess that our world is out of sorts, many have no purpose to the lives that you have created. We ourselves are selfish in our love.
We have hurt your Holy Spirit.
The fruit of the Spirit is patience, kindness and goodness. Father we know that our world is starved of compassion and true friendship. We ourselves can be cruel and hurtful.
We have hurt your Holy Spirit.
The fruit of the Spirit is faithfulness, gentleness and self-control. Father we know that our world is short of truth and justice. We ourselves do not exercise self-control, nor do we let you control us. We give in to weakness and sin.
We have hurt your Holy Spirit.

Word of
assurance: The first verse of 'The Spirit came as promised' (*Psalm Praise*).

Dramatised reading:	Acts 2:1–4, 36 (with children's mime).
Comment:	Say that the friends of Jesus were frightened, but the Holy Spirit came. They heard something amazing come, and they saw something amazing. They felt completely different. They went out from the room where they had been staying and talked freely about Jesus. They weren't frightened any more, and they knew that Jesus was still with them and was still alive. They were very surprised at what was happening.
Song:	Sing 'Jesus loves me' in different languages. Encourage any foreigners to speak of God in their own language, for example, saying, 'Jesus is Lord.'
Comment:	God made it possible for Jesus' friends to use different languages to tell others about him, and he sends his Holy Spirit all over the world today to help people to worship him in their own languages. Jesus didn't speak English, but we can praise God in English or Welsh or French. The disciples would have been surprised to hear people in churches all over the world these days. Instead of being separated by our different languages, the Spirit of God helps us to be united in talking about Jesus.
Testimonies:	Introduce the three people who are to give their testimonies.
Song:	'Holy Spirit will come here'.
Creed	
Prayers:	Include a young child saying simply, 'Thank you, Lord, for the Holy Spirit.'

Song: 'Spirit of the Living God'.

Talk: The Holy Spirit enthuses us and enables us to serve, worship and witness. We have to want and ask for continuing fullness. A singer practises in order not to draw breath in the middle of a line. Marathon runners have to exercise their muscles and lungs to enable their capacity to grow. Those who can't run upstairs are out of condition and must exercise their legs and their lungs to take more air. Similarly we need to practise asking the Spirit to help and enthuse us to speak of Jesus, to worship the Father, to care for others and to let our lives shine. Ask the Holy Spirit to fill you. And ask again, because there'll be more room. You will find yourself changing and doing things you didn't expect.

Hymn: 'Go forth and tell'.

Prayer: Almighty God, you gave the Holy Spirit to the first Christians, making Jesus real to them, teaching them the truth and giving them the power to witness boldly. Fill us with the same Spirit so that we may know their experience and follow their example. Send us out with joy and boldness to witness to your truth and to draw all people to the fire of your love. Through Jesus Christ our Lord. Amen.

Jessie Axtell
Manchester

30   The Holy Spirit: Helper, Guide, Advocate

AIM

To understand the ways in which the Holy Spirit can help each one of us.

TEXT

John 14:16–17a (GNB).

DRAMA

Drama for all the Family 26 'Climbing'.

STORY

'Knave of Hearts Learns to Say Sorry' (Appendix 1.E).

HYMNS

Select from the section dealing with Whitsunday (Pentecost) and the Holy Spirit.

PRAYERS

Prayers for all the Family 51; 52; 200; 371; 395.

MAIN TALK

Preparation

This talk can be illustrated in a variety of ways:

(a) Using objects, namely a football, a mountain map and lawyer's tabs (clerical ones would do!).
(b) Using three people dressed as a football coach, a mountain guide and a lawyer (actually wearing the tabs). These could be interviewed or asked set questions or just be models, depending on the occasion or the people involved.
(c) OHP acetate pictures of the three people described in (b) above.

(In the presentation below it will be assumed that the middle option is taken and all three people are male, seeing that the Bible uses 'he' for the Holy Spirit. Those using another approach, or women models, should make appropriate adjustments.)

Presentation

Explain, possibly by asking leading questions, how before Jesus left his disciples to return to his Father in heaven, he told them to wait in Jerusalem until they received the gift of the Holy Spirit. Jesus knew they could not live the Christian life and witness to him without the help of his Spirit. Earlier in St John's Gospel the Good News Bible translates a difficult Greek word *parakletos*—as 'Helper'. We will consider three ways in which the Holy Spirit can be our Helper.

1. The Holy Spirit as a coach
Introduce your football coach, explaining that he is really a special teacher and discuss with the congregation appropriate questions relating to football skills.

Explain how our trainer Coach, the Holy Spirit, moves us on in our Christian life. He improves our performance. We go forward from being depressed to being encouraged. Our Christian lives will show how the Holy Spirit has been working, if we are willing to allow him to be our Coach.

2. The Holy Spirit as a guide

Bring on your mountain guide, possibly studying a map. He leads us up and on in our climb. If we follow this guide, obeying him and letting him direct us he will move us through difficulties to achievements.

The Holy Spirit is like a mountain guide; he will especially lead us by means of the Bible, which we should study constantly. We can look to him for the way ahead.

3. The Holy Spirit as a lawyer

Bring on your lawyer. The main point to make is that a lawyer can either be counsel for the prosecution or for the defence. The Holy Spirit is rather like a lawyer. He will at times convict us of sin when things are wrong. However he will also defend us before God, acting as our advocate. He will champion us, speak up for us when words fail us, recall that Jesus died for us and paid the price for our sins. The Holy Spirit acts as King's Counsel on behalf of Jesus for each and every Christian.

During the Second World War our famous prime minister, Winston Churchill, looking across to the United States of America, said, 'Give us the tools and we will finish the job.' We also need help to fight the Christian battle, but God has given us our supreme Helper. (Quote text.) The Holy Spirit is truly our Helper as Coach or Teacher, as Guide and as Lawyer or Counsellor.

Ray Adams
Ipsley, Redditch

31   A Talk for Trinity Sunday

AIM

To acknowledge that the doctrine of the Holy Trinity is difficult to understand (as are many things), but that biblical teaching compels us to accept its truth and its wonder.

TEXTS

2 Corinthians 13:13; Ephesians 2:18; 1 Peter 1:2; and the Creed of Saint Athanasius: 'The Father incomprehensible, the Son incomprehensible: and the Holy Ghost incomprehensible.'

DRAMA

Drama for all the Family 27, 'The House with Three Owners'.

HYMNS

See under Holy Trinity especially 'Three-in-One and One-in-Three'. Many hymns have a trinitarian shape, such as 'Lead us, heavenly Father, lead us'.

PRAYERS

Prayers for all the Family 53; 54.

MAIN TALK

Preparation

Attempt to obtain, possibly from a travel agency, some beautiful scenes of the Alps, especially any that include alpine flowers.

Design three OHP acetates to illustrate the three Persons of the Trinity:

God the Father	Creator	creation scene
God the Son	Saviour	the cross
God the Holy Spirit	Strengthener	flames of fire.

Other pictures could be added according to what you are going to include under each heading, eg still waters if you mention Psalm 23; perhaps a heart if you mention God the Father's love.

Presentation

Talk about how either you, or people you know, love climbing in the mountains, especially the Alps and enjoy the magnificent views and flowers, particularly in June and July. It is difficult to remember all their names, but the beauty and wonder will still hit you. Show any pictures you have managed to obtain. In the Alps are several alpine gardens, which are very interesting as all the flowers are labelled. Instead of the riotous beauty of mountains in flower there is order and classification, because the gardens are to help the visitors' understanding.

The Bible tells us much about God the Father, Jesus his Son and the Holy Spirit, but it is all mixed up like alpine flowers in the wild—here one thing and there another.

The *doctrine* (horrible old word, but still a very useful one) of the Trinity is rather like the alpine garden: all is labelled and systematised and visitors can get overwhelmed by all the technical details.

Let us attempt to arrange the different facts about the

Trinity in the Bible, as the wild flowers from the Alps have been put in order in the alpine gardens.

1. God the Father (first OHP acetate)

Refer either to the Apostles' Creed or the baptism creed. Speak of God the Creator as the One who cares for us (Ps 23), as the Father who loves us (cf the Prodigal Son).

2. God the Son (second OHP acetate)

Refer to the Creed. The Gospels tell us very much about Jesus as a Man, as a good teacher and an example. But they also tell us that he is God and our Saviour. Give examples, such as Matthew 1:18–25 and John 1. Refer to the cross.

3. God the Holy Spirit (third OHP acetate)

Refer to the Creed and to the coming of the Spirit at Pentecost in tongues of fire touching each person. Speak about the Spirit who strengthens, enables and empowers us to live the Christian life and to witness to Jesus.

We can enjoy the beauty and wonder of alpine flowers, whether or not we know their names or very much about them. Going to an alpine garden helps us to understand more about them.

So it is with the doctrine of the Trinity. We know God as Creator and loving Father; we know Jesus, God the Son, as Teacher and Saviour; we experience the presence of God the Holy Spirit in our lives. We have difficulty in explaining it, but just as we can experience the wonder of wild flowers without knowing all their names, so we can experience God as Trinity without fully understanding it.

Repeat main headings and possibly end with the Grace from 2 Corinthians 13:13.

Michael Roberts
Chirk, Clwyd

The Christian Life

32   Election!

AIM

To illustrate the eternal and unbreakable character of God's love for us. (This talk would be most effective if it took place just before, or just after, an election, local or national.)

TEXT

Ephesians 1:1–10.

HYMNS

'Dear Lord and Father of mankind'; 'Father of heaven, whose love profound'; 'Praise my soul, the King of heaven'.

PRAYERS

Prayers for all the Family (Forgiveness) 28; 388; 405; (Parliament) 351; 368.

MAIN TALK

Preparation

You will need two cardboard boxes with a slit, to represent ballot boxes. Slips of paper marked as ballot papers.

A strong 'soap box', perhaps with 'soap' painted on the side, strong enough to stand on.

Presentation

The talk could begin with a humorous introduction about politicians getting on their 'high horses' at election time, and how clergy *never* do this. At which point someone might rather ostentatiously bring in the soap box and put it down in front of you. Climb on to it, and proceed to hold a suitable mock election—perhaps for the next Vicar/Minister, or whatever. If that is too close to home, try something more innocuous in church life. If you are brave, you might even try to identify the issues in an actual election which is to take place, or has just taken place. You might arrange for two or three candidates to give one- or two-minute election addresses, and then ask a reasonable number of people (a dozen or so, perhaps) to cast their votes into one of the ballot boxes.

These election addresses could be kept fairly humorous, or thought could be given to embodying a message through them (selfishness, short-term thinking, etc). It is often an ideal way of involving uninhibited teenagers in worship. (Is there a religious equivalent to the Monster-Raving-Loony party?!)

While your electors are casting their votes, and the votes are being counted, talk about the way elections are commonly conducted, with candidates making promises they find hard to keep, etc. If the election addresses have embodied serious messages, reflect upon them. Then announce the verdict in the mock election.

At this point, produce the second ballot box, with either 'God' or 'The Bible' written on the side, and open it to reveal just one ballot paper with either 'love' or 'forgiveness' and a tick alongside. Proceed to talk about how the Bible reveals a God who keeps his promises, and freely chooses to offer us love and forgiveness in his victory in Jesus Christ—which doesn't just last until the next time an election comes round, but for all eternity. Indeed, God chose to love us in Jesus Christ before the world was even made (Eph 1:4).

All we are required to do is to believe the promises, and to be prepared to join his 'party'—both to campaign for him as we are able to, and to celebrate his unshakeable victory.

Peter Forster
Beverley Minster

33   A New Creation

Aim

To illustrate some aspects of new life in Christ and how to receive it.

Text

2 Corinthians 5:11–21.

Drama

Drama for all the Family 31, 'Home Improvements'; *Scenes and Wonders* (Appendix 2) p 41 'Good News'.

Hymns

'Firmly I believe and truly'; 'God forgave my sin in Jesus' name'; 'How sweet the name of Jesus sounds'; 'I am trusting you, Lord Jesus'; 'I want to walk with Jesus Christ'; 'Just as I am, without one plea'.

Prayers

Prayers for all the Family 22; 56; 188; 243.

MAIN TALK

Preparation

You will need a cabbage. Also have an OHP acetate with a caterpillar and a butterfly depicted on it and the words 'New life in Christ Jesus' printed on it. If an OHP is not available have it all depicted on a large card.

Presentation

Why have I brought a cabbage with me? What possible use is it? Invite answers (to eat, use as a football, etc).

Well, I want to do a 'Once upon a time' story that involves the cabbage. It's about a brother and sister, Christopher and Karen, part of a very big family, the Caterpillars, who lived on cabbage. They were a very happy family; life was good and they felt very pleased with the way things were on their own cabbage.

But one day things changed. They became very sleepy and just couldn't stay awake any longer.

'Goodnight Karen,' said Christopher.

'Goodnight Christopher,' said Karen.

When they woke up they felt very strange.

'Is that you, Karen?'

'I think so, but I'm not sure. I feel different.'

'You look different, too.'

'So do you.'

Instead of long chubby bodies with lots of legs and great big jaws for munching cabbage, they were transformed!

Use the illustrations on the OHP acetate or card to show the transformation. Stress the beauty of the butterfly.

Now Karen and Christopher could fly! They could see there was a whole world beyond their cabbage and they weren't interested in that old life any more.

Refer to 2 Corinthians 5:11–21.

'If anyone is in Christ, he is a new creation, the old has

gone, the new has come' (verse 17). That is the promise God makes to us—new life in Christ. How?

'He [Jesus] died for all' (verse 15).

'God made him who had no sin to be sin for us, so that in him we might become the righteousness of God' (verse 21).

What a promise! How exciting that we, with all our faults, can become the righteousness of God.

'We implore you on Christ's behalf, be reconciled to God' (verse 20).

Let him give us wings, the beauty of a butterfly. Let's not stay caterpillars—let's receive the new life Christ offers. Then we can be some use in the world. We can live for him who died for us (verse 15). We can become ambassadors for Christ (verse 20), spreading the good news of new life in Christ.

Let us pray. Lord we want to accept the gift you offer— to be a new creation. Thank you for Jesus. Help us now to serve him. Amen.

Patricia Chowney
Horsell, Woking

34   What a Load of Rubbish!

AIM

To show that God will forgive and help us to overcome our sinful nature.

TEXTS

Genesis 4:2–8; Isaiah 44:22.

DRAMA

Drama for all the Family 56 'The Rich Fool'.

STORY

'The Upside Down Men' (Appendix 1.R); 'White Lies' (Appendix 1.F).

HYMNS

'Amazing grace!'; 'And can it be'; 'Glory be to Jesus'; 'Man of sorrows! what a name'; 'There is a green hill far away'.

PRAYERS

Prayers for all the Family 2; 21; 76; 214; 251; 406.

Main Talk

Preparation

You will need empty packets and tins, egg boxes, jars, etc, with words on them, such as 'thoughtlessness', 'unkind words', 'unkind thoughts', 'selfishness', 'laziness', 'impatience', 'bad language', 'jealousy', etc on. These can be hidden around the church or placed in a large cardboard box.

A large black plastic bin bag will be needed, and a small roll of bin liners with the words 'anger', 'resentment', 'hatred', 'lies', 'deviousness'—one word on each bin bag. Don't separate them. Leave them still joined at the perforations and roll up the bags again.

Presentation

What I am going to talk about this morning is a complete load of rubbish! (This will probably produce a murmur of 'not unusual'!) Talk about the rubbish we have in our everyday lives. What's in a lady's handbag? Those bits of wire, string and nails that men collect and never use. The torn comics, dried-up felt-tip pens and broken toys that children hold on to, and as soon as Mum wants to throw them out they're the only things the kids play with for the next few days! We hoard rubbish. Twenty million tons of it are cleared from our homes every year by the binmen or 'cleansing engineers' as they are sometimes known. It takes only one month to create our own weight in rubbish. What a mess! What trouble is caused when rubbish is not collected and properly disposed of. How quickly, in a binmen strike, the sacks of household rubbish pile up and begin to cause a health hazard as they rot and smell and the rats come. We are very fortunate that in this country we have safe and regular disposal of our rubbish.

But you know, there is all sorts of rubbish in our spiritual lives and that needs safe and regular disposal too.

Our thoughtlessness	'Yes, I know I said I'd ring you but there was a good programme on telly and then I was too tired.'
Our unkind words	'You're pathetic at football! That drawing is stupid!'
Our unkind thoughts	'I hope she gets spots for going out with that boy I fancied!'
Our selfishness	'It's my ball so we'll play the game I want!'

These parts of us are the sin, the rubbish that we must make an effort to throw out. What we need is a big black bin sack to collect it all up. Now I happen to know that there is *a lot* of rubbishy sin around here and I'm going to collect it in. . . .

Invite people, young and old, to find the 'rubbish' that you have hidden, or ask them to come and take something out of the large box.

So, here we are with a bag of sin rubbish. What do we do with it? We give it to God, ask him to deal with all these sins in our life, remembering that Jesus died on the cross for our sin and in the power of the Holy Spirit we can strive to overcome sin. But there's a problem with rubbish . . .

Rubbish keeps accumulating. It sneaks up on you like your household rubbish does. For instance, when you've had a good clear out of the kitchen cupboards, the toy box or the garden shed everything seems neat and tidy, but before very long yet *another* clear out is needed. That's why regularly in our worship we have a time of prayer asking for God to forgive us the wrong we keep doing and to help us lead new lives.

These bin bags come on a roll. They are all joined together. Sin is like that. It is said that 'sin knows nothing of addition, only multiplication'. In other words, one sin leads to another. Anger becomes resentment; lying leads to deviousness; selfishness brings out greed and cheating. Remember our reading. Cain was envious, jealous of Abel. His envy became resentment; his resentment turned to hatred; and that hatred led to murder.

So, the next time you have to empty the waste-paper basket and put out the bin sacks for the cleansing engineers, think about getting rid of the sin, the wrong things in your life. Thank and praise God that he *will* forgive us the wrong things we do if we turn to him and truly repent. It is there in Isaiah 44:22: 'I have swept away your offences like a cloud, your sins like the morning mist. Return to me, for I have redeemed you.'

Jane Parry
Crowton, Cheshire

35   Every Loser Wins

AIM

Using Jesus' most famous parable of the Prodigal Son to
challenge us to be winners with him, not losers without
him.

T<small>EXT</small>

Luke 15:11–32; see also *The Dramatised Bible*, p 167,
New Testament section.

D<small>RAMA</small>

Drama for all the Family 57 'The Prodigal Daughter'.

H<small>YMNS</small>

'Amazing grace!'; 'Father of heaven, whose love profound'; 'God made me for himself, to serve him here';
'O Jesus, I have promised'; 'The King of love my Shepherd is'.

P<small>RAYERS</small>

Prayers for all the Family 21; 76; 77–87 (Chapter of
Confessions); 101–108 (Litanies of Confession).

Main Talk

Preparation

Use either a teazlegraph board or OHP acetates to put up the words in CAPITALS, as illustrated.

Presentation

Part 1

Refer to the TV advert for the Prudential Insurance Company in which various people say, 'I wanna be rich . . . drive a Porsche . . . be a slug!'

In the reading the younger son wanted to get away from the farm, to get his inheritance early, to enjoy life and do all the things rich people did. At the beginning of the story he really did look as if he was A WINNER (put up on left under HE LOOKED LIKE).

Put up HE HAD and under it put up the following words, commenting as vividly as possible on each: MONEY, FRIENDS, FOOD, SELF-RESPECT.

He really looked like a winner . . . but, the Bible story tells us, he was really A LOSER (put up on right under HE WAS), not a winner.

We are told he was OUT OF HIS SENSES (put under A LOSER). The money he had went to his head and he couldn't think straight. Many people, who have won great fortunes, have blown the lot and ruined their lives. The National Lottery is likely to have the same effect on future winners' lives.

He hurt people, especially his father, who waited longingly for his return. He had NO LOVE (put up on right) for anyone, except himself, and the things that money could buy. He may have appeared very much alive, but under the mask he was DEAD (put up on right). Eventually his money ran out, and with it his friends, food and self-respect (put up NO in front of MONEY, FRIENDS,

FOOD and SELF-RESPECT). He ended up with a very poorly paid job and pig-swill to eat—awful, especially for a Jewish boy. Yeuch!

Part 2

At last he CAME TO HIS (replace OUT OF HIS) SENSES. He suddenly realised what a fool he had been. He now realised his father's workers were getting better food than he was. He decided he would go home and ask his father's forgiveness. Saying sorry is very difficult at times, especially when we have hurt someone. The son might not have been taken back, but he thought he'd give it a go.

He really looked like a LOSER . . . but really he was a WINNER (exchange WINNER with LOSER). He realised what was important in life—and it wasn't money and parties.

He saw his father and he suddenly realised he had great love for him (remove the NO from before LOVE). His father forgave him and threw a great feast in his son's honour. He was no longer DEAD but ALIVE (replacing DEAD).

Jesus told this story to show what we are like and what God is like. We are sometimes out of our senses and get things wrong. Just like the younger son we walk away from our heavenly Father. We might think things are all right and that we are winners, but whenever we walk away from God we are always losers.

The father in the story WAITED (put at bottom central) patiently for the son to return to him. God is WAITING (replacing WAITED) for each one of us, whatever age we are to come to our senses, to come with sorrow for our sin and selfishness and confess, and so have a real relationship with him. He is waiting to celebrate with each of us when we do come to him . . . and there is a party in heaven

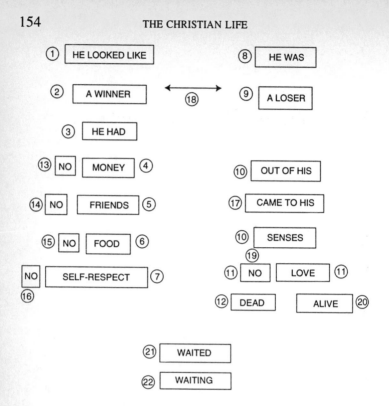

when anyone gives their lives to him and puts Jesus at the centre of their lives.

When this happens every LOSER becomes a WINNER.

God challenges us today to be WINNERS, not LOSERS.

Peter Hall
Bromyard, Herefordshire

36   Being Like Children

To explore the meaning of Jesus' call to become like children, encouraging children to be aware of the possibility of their knowing God, and persuading adults not to be deceived by their supposed sophistication.

TEXT

Matthew 18:1–4.

HYMNS

'Jesus, good above all other'; Once in royal David's city'.

PRAYERS

Prayers for all the Family 252; (on humility) 63, 243, 341.

MAIN TALK

Preparation

The illustration shows the sketches which are to be drawn while the talk is in progress. This is far easier than one might suppose. The key is to do all the drawing beforehand, but with faint pencil lines, and to over-draw the lines with felt pens while speaking.

155

The preliminary pencil-work should also include reminders of the order in which the details of the sketches are to be over-drawn and of the colours to be used. Thus the illustrations have '(1) blue', etc. The use of different colours not only adds brightness, but also gives continuity, because each character keeps his own colour throughout the story.

The equipment required comprises an A1 size flip-chart pad, a board to which the pad may be clipped, an easel, and felt pens of medium thickness.

It is recommended that the adult figures be drawn about eight inches in height, and the child figures about five inches. Also, sufficient time should be spent in achieving suitable postures for the figures. (This becomes easier with practice!)

Much of the text consists of questions, so let the congregation suggest answers, and become involved in the unfolding story.

Presentation

Introduction

Children are for ever being told to 'grow up', but I want to give exactly the opposite advice! And I am on safe ground because Jesus did the same, as we heard in the reading.

Let's think about what he must have meant.

Sheet 1

Draw (1). Where do you think he's going in such a hurry? I'll give you a clue.

Draw (2).

Draw (3) (without the bag). More dashing about! Where to now?

Draw (4).

Draw (5). This is my friend William. What do you think he is doing?

Draw (6). He's not in a rush. He's got time to stop and look. We give time to stop, look at God's written word, and to listen to what God is saying to us. Have you got time for God?

Sheet 2

Draw (1). O dear, big trouble! But see what happened next day.

Draw (2). What are William and his friend doing now? What has happened between them?

Draw (3). Now what's going on here? Let's see what they did next day.

Draw (4). Typical! Don't they look silly! Adults find it so hard to forgive.

We are learning to be more like young William and his friend. Jesus is teaching us to forgive. And to receive forgiveness, from each other, but first from God.

Sheet 3

Draw (1). Here's William again. He's agitated about something. Let's see what it is.

Draw (2). Hey, that's marvellous. He can see the heavenly city, and I think he can just hear the singing too. But I wonder why he is so agitated. He should be happy, and joining in the singing too. I'll put the missing piece in the picture.

Draw (3). There's the problem. One of those adults again! William is trying to tell him about the heavenly city, and he won't even look!

We are learning to be less adult. We regularly look at the heavenly city, and we join in the singing too. Do join us.

Philip Manning
Langdale, Cumbria

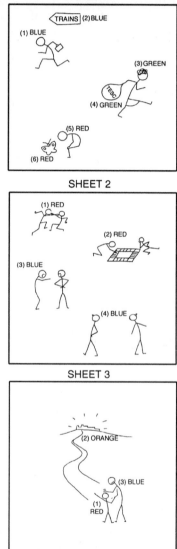

37 The Five Ls of Family Life (Also Suitable for Mothering Sunday)

AIM

To encourage family members to see how their faith can illuminate their family life—and vice versa.

TEXT

1 John 4:16.

DRAMA

Drama for all the Family 17 'Happy Families'.

HYMNS

'For the beauty of the earth'; 'Happy the home that welcomes you, Lord Jesus'; 'Loving Shepherd of your sheep'; 'There's a song for all the children'. Some hymn books have a Marriage, Home and Children's section.

PRAYERS

Prayers for all the Family 68; 96; 111 (Litany); 131; 199; 230; 237; 239; 242; 244; 247; 250; 283–287. See also Section 2 on Family Prayers at Home, from which some of these prayers come.

159

Main Talk

Preparation

Design, or get an imaginative artist to do so, five OHP acetates to illustrate the five Ls below, with which to introduce each section, eg a green L plate for the fifth.

Presentation

Begin with a number of personalised humorous stories about the reality of family life, possibly illustrated by Mothering Sunday cards. When the Editor saw this talk given, Mrs Munn, when dealing with the second L below, told of the occasion when she entered her teenage son's bedroom, and commented about the state it was in. She was physically picked up and placed outside the room, to the considerable amusement of both mother and son!

Ask what the connection is between these and our faith. Offer the five Ls which make the connection:

1. Living with failure

No one is perfect: no family, no parent (worth mentioning the concept of the 'good enough' parent—D.W. Winnicott—see Appendix 2). Christians are prone to live with guilt and to feel they have failed. It is important to remember that Christ himself experienced failure—rejection, misunderstanding, crucifixion—and that he is present in our failure as well as our success. We need to experience failure in order to experience resurrection hope. When we share our vulnerability with God and with our family and friends, we become closer. Christians know how forgiveness heals (eg in the parable of the Prodigal Son and the Forgiving Father) and is an essential part of living with failure.

2. Letting go

Christian family life is often perceived as rigid. One of the hardest things for parents to manage is to allow appropriate freedom for children—and ultimately to let them go. This applies to other relationships too. God gives us free will (cf Prodigal Son).

3. *Listening*

We are made in the image of a listening God. When we are listened to, we feel accepted, valued, special—what a gift to offer one another! Listening is not easy, but it is a skill which can be learned. Through listening we show mutual respect. 'Submit yourselves to one another because of your reverence for Christ' (Eph 5:21). Encouragement is part of listening 'Do not use harmful words but helpful ones' (Eph 4:29).

4. *Love*

Love needs to be understood as meaning more than just feelings. The family is the 'school of love' (Martin Luther). All humans need experience of unconditional love and acceptance like that we experience from God. 'Love without strings' is the love needed but often our pride gets in the way. 'Those who live in love live in God and God lives in them' (1 Jn 3:24).

5. *Learning*

L plate (for new driver) can illustrate this, symbolising the activity of the Holy Spirit, the agent of growth and change. Family life requires constant adjustment and will-ingness to grow. We are all learners on the journey of family life. (Use green L plate rather than red—there are no exams to pass in family life!)

Tricia Munn
Family Life and Marriage Education Adviser,
Diocese of Chester

38   The Pressures on Young People

To challenge the congregation in their understanding of the pressures on young people, God's love for them and the need for adults to follow God's example of showing them love also.

N<small>OTE</small>

Mrs Chantry has specifically told the Editor that she does not regard this as a Family Service talk, and that it is probably unsuitable for children under eleven. Someone else, who has seen the talk given, would reduce the age to eight.

Perhaps there should be some ministerial guidance here. When the Editor saw the talk given he noted the rapt attention of all ages, not least the teenagers, and the talk was spontaneously applauded. It is unashamedly included in this book.

T<small>EXT</small>

Luke 2:41–52 (see *The Dramatised Bible* p 126 New Testament section).

DRAMA

Scenes and Wonders (Appendix 2) 'The First Church', pp 32–35; *Ten Minute Miracle Plays* (Appendix 2) 'Jesus in the Temple', pp 115–119.

HYMNS

'I'm accepted, I'm forgiven'; 'Just as I am, without one plea'; 'Shine, Jesus, shine'.

PRAYERS

Prayers for all the Family 162–164.

MAIN TALK

Preparation

A selection of items which represent young people's lives and the pressures on them: eg Doc Marten's, jeans, tee shirt (so that you can make out a unisex teenager shape), Walkman-style headphones (for the head), schoolfile/ book, CDs, computer game box, teenage magazine, make-up bag/bottle of spot lotion, razor and tampax box, cheque book, tablespoon of sugar wrapped in cling- film (or a needle), condom, cider bottle, video box, cigar- ette packet and small mirror. You will also need a small candle and matches.

Presentation

It would make the Bible much simpler if it were a text book and we could look up a subject in the index at the back and discover the pages that dealt with how to handle some of the pressures on young people today. We could discover where to find out about exam tension, raves or grunge.

However the Bible was written for a different culture. So we need to look first at the pressures on young people and see what God has to say to them in their situation. It is interesting that in the only story we have of Jesus as an adolescent his parents didn't understand him!

We need to build up a picture of what it is like to be a teenager today by looking at some of the things normally in the possession of many modern young people.

Proceed to build up a picture by producing the different items you have collected. Talk about peer pressure, the assumptions of TV and the media about honesty, sex, sexuality, family, etc. This may be seen as stereotyping young people, so it is important to state that not all young people are the same—they are individuals—but these are the general pressures on them. The mirror represents the question which is underlying all adolescence: 'Who am I? Not just my parents' child. What do I think and believe?'

Our reading is a reminder that God became a human being, to bring light (light candle and place next to the articles shown above); to bring good news to all people, including young people.

Is the gospel good news for young people?
The gospel is often confused by those outside the church with 'church' and therefore not an attractive option. We drive up in our big cars (ecologically dodgy), wear our smart clothes (conformist and middle class), and are seen as patronising to young people and plain boring!

The gospel is good news for young people
What is specifically good news for them? Acceptance as they are, love to the unlovely, forgiveness, new life, new opportunities, even a new family! New purpose, opportunities to belong and be involved, to develop gifts and to

know peace and joy. God gives huge responsibilities to the young: eg Joseph, Samuel, David, Daniel, Mary, Timothy. In the gospel stories Jesus takes people seriously without patronising them: no 'Come back when you're older.' Young people have a part to play in the body of Christ *now*.

Our responsibility to young people as Christians

If we talk of the church as a family then we all have a huge responsibility for our young people—people with their own identity (rather than 'John's son'), a responsibility to those who feel excluded from society, those who have no voice today, the young unemployed, the young homeless, the abused, the drug users, those who feel unloved and unwanted, those who take to crime or go on 'the game' because they see it as the only way to survive. We need to campaign on their behalf, as well as care for those we meet. They are not somebody else's problem. Remember the Children's Society poster 'What I need is a good listening to'? They need space to grow from children to adults, a chance to develop gifts.

Not legalism but loyalty

Teenagers cannot be forced to do anything, so we need to operate with them in ways of co-operation. Our responsibility is to be good stewards, whether as parents, God-parents, friends or brothers and sisters in Christ, to help them grow into responsible adulthood, so that they can make good decisions for themselves.

Ten Commandments for those who have, or work with, young people

1. You shall love them at all times, even when they drive you mad!

2. You shall remember that you are God's stewards of them and not be possessive.

3. You shall think of them as 'almost adult' rather than children.

4. You shall respect their need for privacy. They will decide when they want to share their secrets with you.

5. You shall give them responsibility and freedom, foster loyalty rather than laying down the law, and support them in the mistakes they make.

6. You shall be available to be a listening ear, without being offended if they choose someone else. Be interested without being the Inquisition!

7. You shall learn to say sorry and admit mistakes, for how will they learn, if they don't see you doing it?

8. You shall develop a 'nag free' zone, or they will create their own in a place where you can't find them!

9. You shall not covet your offspring's youth, but look for the positive things of your own age.

10. You shall pray and support them at all times and encourage them in all they do.

Helen Chantry
Joint Youth Officer
Diocese of Chester

This talk is based round a meditation devised by the Revd Jane Scott, Youth Leadership Training Officer for the URC for North West and Merseyside.

39 How to Have a Beautiful Body

AIM

To teach about the church, the body of Christ.

Text

1 Corinthians 12:12–27.

DRAMA

Drama for all the Family has two sketches on this theme: 38 'Bodywork' and 39 'The Cake'. See also *Divine Comedies* (Appendix 2) 'Body Language' pp 102–105, but note Nigel Forde's comments on p. 101.

STORY

'Jasper, Caspar and George' (Appendix 1.S); 'The Story of Two People Who Went to Church' (Appendix 1.T).

HYMNS

See Church section of hymn book. Also 'Bind us together, Lord'; 'For I'm building a people of power' (*Songs of Fellowship* 43 and 111).

PRAYERS

Prayers for all the Family 57; 147; 148; 156; 211; 250.

MAIN TALK

Preparation

You will need a music group, which must be properly rehearsed beforehand. Also prepare an OHP acetate with the four points made in the talk.

Presentation

Take one. Explain we are going to sing a song that speaks about belonging to the body of Christ, the church. Begin to play (eg 'Bind us together'). They have the right music, all in tune, but each is playing a different song, in a different key.

Explain that church can be a bit like that. All the right ingredients are present, but everyone is not pulling in the same direction. *All of us are in one body*. Not just held together by a common interest or faith, but actually in Christ—united in him. His life, the Holy Spirit, runs through all of us, like blood running through all parts of a body.

Take two. Try the song once again. This time one member of the group plays a solo. When challenged they reply that they just like doing their own thing.

In the church there is no place for soloists. The body is *made up of many parts* (verse 14). No one person is more important, not even the vicar. Christ is the Head and no one else. Living the Christian life is a corporate activity— you don't get far doing it by yourself. You need the support of others. It's better to play in a band than be a soloist.

Take three. Return to the song. During your previous explanation, the group have swapped instruments. Each is now trying to play someone else's instrument. After challenging them, they reply that they always wanted to play something else and would much rather be someone else, etc.

We might envy each other's gifts and opportunities or strengths, but *God put us together as he wanted* (verse 18). Each of us is given a gift or role or calling by God and each of us is called to be ourselves in the context of each other. We all have something to offer.

Take four. Return to the song. During the last bit of the talk one member of the group has sidled off discreetly and is now playing cards at the back of the church. When challenged they reply that they don't feel wanted or they're not needed or important, etc.

God values each of us equally. *We cannot do without even those parts that seem weaker* (verses 22 and 23). God looks at who we are, not what we do. Even those parts which feel they have less to offer are valuable—eg, the importance of a little finger to grip or a little toe to walk, etc.

Take five. Sing the song through together with no fooling around.

Conclude by getting the congregation to say aloud the four points made by way of a statement of what the church is like.

Mike Burke
Sheffield

40 Belonging to God and His Church

AIM

To teach the meaning of belonging to God in terms of privilege and responsibility.

TEXT

1 Peter 2:9 (NIV).

DRAMA

Scenes and Wonders (Appendix 2) 'Holiday Camp' pp 36–40.

STORY

'Jasper, Caspar and George' (Appendix 1.S); 'The Story of Two People Who Went to Church' (Appendix 1.T).

HYMNS

'Church of God, elect and glorious'; 'Glorious things of you are spoken'; 'You that know the Lord is gracious'.

PRAYERS

Prayers for all the Family 57; 147; 148; 156; 211; 250.

MAIN TALK

Preparation

Five objects are needed:
    football (or rugby depending on the area!) supporter's
        scarf
    school tie
    clerical collar
    neckerchief as worn by Scouts, Guides, etc.
    wedding ring.

Presentation

Show the objects in the order listed above. After the fourth one, ask what they all have in common. An answer of 'They are all worn around the neck' may be expected. Show the fifth object, which clearly isn't worn around the neck—so this can't be the right answer. Draw out the answer 'They all represent belonging.' Go through objects again explaining this.

Supporter's scarf—only worn by those who belong to the group of supporters for a particular team.

School tie—only worn by those who belong to a particular school.

Clerical collar—only worn by those belonging to a particular profession.

Neckerchief—only worn by those belonging to a troop, pack, unit, etc.

Wedding ring—expression of vows—husband and wife belonging to each other.

Just as we belong to groups, so those who profess to be Christians belong to God (1 Pet 2:9) because he claims them as his own. 1 Peter 2:10 reminds us that once we didn't belong to God. We probably all know what it's like to feel left out (elaborate on this with examples). God doesn't want us to feel like this but to respond to his love for us shown in the person of Jesus and to acknowledge that we belong to him.

These same symbols can help us remember what it means to belong to God:

Scarf—support by keeping in touch with God especially through prayer and worship and Bible reading.

Tie—learn what God wants for us, which is always the best.

Collar—belonging to God involves being active in a job for him.

Neckerchief—worn by uniformed organisation across the world—a sign of unity. There are millions of others who belong to God—a great encouragement.

Ring—self-giving and commitment—no holding back anything.

Belonging to God involves a great deal in terms of privilege and responsibility. All is possible if we really want to belong to him.

Chris Bracegirdle
Astley, Manchester

41   Running the Christian Race

AIM

To enlarge on the popular biblical theme of the Christian life being a race.

TEXT

Hebrews 12:1–3.

DRAMA

Drama for all the Family 26 (not on running but has parallels with the theme).

HYMNS

'Fight the good fight'; 'O Jesus, I have promised'.

PRAYERS

Prayers for all the Family 15; 29; 408; 409.

MAIN TALK

Preparation

You will need to prepare a series of OHP acetates, with the pictures carefully placed, in order to build up a composite picture by gradually super-imposing one after another, as illustrated.

Presentation

What games do you like? Anyone play football? Cricket? Tiddlywinks? Anyone do running? The Christian life is like a race, and we need to be sure we run it in the right way. (Acetate 1 of runner.) The Bible says, 'So run that you may obtain' (1 Cor 9:24). How should we run in order to be sure of winning a prize? Here are four hot tips on how to run the race.

1. *'Witnesses'* (verse 1) (Acetate 2, onlookers.)
These are not just spectators, onlookers, but those who have run the race before, and who can give us advice, like a trainer, or a famous runner. Do you have a hero you model yourself on? Do you have his or her picture on your bedroom wall?

The Bible gives us advice and examples of people to follow in the race of the Christian life. (Acetate 3, Bible, and word LEARN.) We need to read it, and not just read it, but to take note of it, to learn it. It may be hard, but it's helpful. You can't afford not to read it if you want to win the race.

2. *'Throw off'* (verse 1)
This means there are some things that we have to leave behind. (Acetate 4, syringe and word LEAVE.) There are two kinds of things we have to leave.

There are *forbidden things*, like drugs (hence the syringe), what the verse calls 'sins'. The Ten Commandments, for example, tell us about some of these. The Bible tells us we have got to run 'according to the rules' (2 Tim 2:5).

There are also *unhelpful things*, like for example running in big heavy boots. (Acetate 5 of boots.) These things are not necessarily forbidden, but they hinder me from running well. In the first Olympics runners were

Complete Picture

naked for this reason. Present-day athletic wear is so small competitors are almost naked! Like weighing in at the airport, there's a limit to the luggage of life. Otherwise we don't get off the ground!

3. 'Perseverance' (verse 1)
This means to last out to the end. (Acetate 6, rainbow, and word LAST.) In the race of the Christian life, this means lasting out until we see God on his rainbow-circled throne in heaven. It's a long-distance race. Don't get sidetracked. People say Christianity is just 'kids' stuff', and you grow out of it when you get older; it's not for 'real men'. So how come some of the Brazil world cup winning football team were Christians? You would hardly call them wimps! Keep on keeping on. There are no quick fixes and short cuts; 'stickability' is the name of the game.

4. 'Fix your eyes on Jesus' (verse 2)
Look to Jesus. (Acetate 7, cross and word LOOK.) In a race, if you look over your shoulder at someone else, or if you look around, you can lose ground, even lose the race. Peter, walking on the water, began to sink when he took his eyes off Jesus. In Rubens' picture of the Last Supper, all the disciples are shown intently gazing at Jesus; except Judas.

How can we 'see' him? Verse 3 says 'consider'—think about him. (Acetate 8, thought symbols.) Think about Jesus; how he suffered on the cross and then went to heaven. 'Lest you grow weary' (verse 3)—this will help you last out to the end.

There are four hot tips on how to run the race of the Christian life — LEARN, LEAVE, LAST and LOOK. Do you run like that? Is that the way you live your life?

Bernard Baker
Ryde, Isle of Wight

42 Calling Disciples

AIM

To show that you don't have to be anyone special to serve Jesus.

TEXT

Mark 1:14–20.

DRAMA

Drama for all the Family 29 'The Non-Hallowe'en Party'. This may seem a strange sketch to recommend, but we are all called to be saints and all saints should be disciples. Also *Sketches from Scripture* (Appendix 2) 'Recruitment', pp 54–57.

STORY

'Jasper, Caspar and George' (Appendix 1.S).

HYMNS

'Dear Lord and Father of mankind'; 'I'm special'; 'I want to walk with Jesus Christ'; 'Jesus calls us! o'er the tumult'.

PRAYERS

Prayers for all the Family 5; 51; 52; 65; 149; 196.

MAIN TALK

Preparation

You will need ten cards with letters on as described.

Presentation

Imagine there's a group of teenagers in a church youth group and we need to choose some of them to train as Sunday school teachers. We need help in deciding who's suitable.

Ask for volunteers to hold up the cards with letters on. Describe the character of each member of the group but don't give away their real names at this stage.

1. A—SHY

A (Andrew) is quiet and shy. He brings others along but doesn't like taking the lead.

2. P—NOT VERY BRIGHT

P (Philip) is a Christian but he doesn't know the Bible very well, and he doesn't really understand some basic Christian teaching.

3. J—DISHONEST

J (Judas Iscariot) has been looking after the youth group's funds but he's been helping himself to them. He's generally a trouble maker.

4. T—NEVER SURE

T (Thomas) is always full of questions. He's not easily convinced. He's been arguing recently about the physical resurrection of Jesus.

5. L—KEEN CHURCHGOER

L (Levite) comes to lots of services with his parents. He's grown up in the church family. He knows lots of Bible stories.

6. J AND J—NOISY AND GREEDY

J and J (James and John, sons of thunder) are nicknamed 'the Loud Bangs' because they are so noisy! You always know when they're around. They are ambitious and want to be in on everything and have the best places.

7. M—UNPOPULAR, NOT TRUSTED

M (Matthew) got a job straight from school in the local council offices. He's very keen on his work there collecting the council tax. Some people think he gets a rake-off. No one trusts him, he's very unpopular.

8. P—GOOD AT RE

P (Priest) is very clever. He got 'A' at GCSE in RE. He always does well in any Bible quiz.

9. S—BLUNT AND TALKATIVE

S (Simon) is impetuous and chatty. He says just what he thinks . . . the first thing that comes into his head! He's always opening his mouth and putting his foot in it!

10. B, J, S AND T—QUIET ONES

B (Bartholomew)

J (James, son of Alphaeus)

S (Simon the Zealot)

T (Thaddaeus/ or Judas, Son of James)

A nondescript little group of friends. There's nothing special to say about them. They don't volunteer to take a lead and you don't notice them much.

Go along the row and decide: which would you give a tick to and which would you give a cross to? Discuss the choices. Then alter the ticks and crosses around as necessary to show the choices Jesus made.

Jesus *didn't* choose clever, 'religious' people—no priests, Levites, scribes or Pharisees.

Jesus *did* choose ordinary people with doubts,

questions, faults and failings, to be his followers and to train and tell others about him.

So Jesus could be calling anyone here today. Might he be calling you?

Sheila Lloyd
Braintree

43 The Twofold Command to Love

AIM

To explore the twofold nature of Jesus' new commandment.

TEXT

Matthew 22:34–40.

DRAMA

Drama for all the Family 46 'God's Love is Like . . .'; 41 'Love is . . .'.

STORY

In January 1956, five missionaries who had been seeking to bring the Christian gospel to the Auca Indians (a savage, stoneage tribe, in the heart of Equador) were speared to death. Ten years later, in 1966, some of the Auca converts to Christianity, including Kimo, one of the killers, visited Britain to tell of the change that the risen Lord had brought into their lives. They had been won over by the love and dedication of the closest relations of the martyred missionaries. Women like Elizabeth Elliot and Rachel Saint refused to let their bereavement make them bitter. They determined to press on in the attempt to reach these ignorant tribesmen with the good news. They went to live and labour among them, and in due time the selfless love which radiated out from these dedicated women won the majority of this small tribe to Christ. Interestingly enough, the first to come to faith among the Aucas were the men who actually did the killings. One of them, Gikita, said simply, 'I used to hate and kill but now the Lord has healed my heart.' Such is their love for others, such their concern to pass on to others the gospel that has made new men of them, that they are now risking their lives to tell of the Saviour to a neighbouring tribe of Indians, with whom they have had a blood feud from time immemorial. (*Man Alive!* by Michael Green [IVP 1992].)

HYMNS

See section of hymn book that deals with Love and Devotion. Probably the best-known examples are 'Love divine, all loves excelling' and 'The King of love my Shepherd is'.

PRAYERS

Prayers for all the Family 44; 58; 60; 201; 214; 240; 252.

MAIN TALK

Preparation

Make a large heart at least one metre across—one half marked 'Love God', the other half marked 'Love your neighbour'.

Make a lot of small hearts (about 15 cm across) with similar wording and cut them in half.

Make cardboard letters L-O-V-E.

Presentation

Children ask a lot of *why* questions. Give examples and discuss. Some of these can be very deliberately light-hearted. As Christians we never stop asking 'Why?':

Why did God make the world?

Why did God send Jesus?

A major part of the answer to these questions lies in the word LOVE. Ask four children to come out and hold the letters.

God loves us so much he sent his Son, Jesus. Jesus loves us so much he died for us.

As Christians we respond to that love God has for us with our love for him.

What should that love be like?

Ask all the children out to the front and give them half a heart on which is written 'Love God'. Talk about the importance of this but explain that it is not the full story. Ask if they want to be half-hearted Christians! Send them around the church to find the other half of their heart previously hidden.

When they come back with the two pieces make an activity of showing one piece, with the other behind the back, and then the reverse, to learn what it means to love God, but not be bothered about neighbours and vice versa. Then bring out the large heart as the children hold the two parts of their hearts together.

There are two parts to Jesus' new commandment and we cannot be whole-hearted in our witness and discipleship if both parts are not active in our lives.

Betty Pedley
Parish Education Adviser
Diocese of Wakefield

44　Evergreen Christians

To show that a healthy Christian life results from staying in regular contact with God.

Texts

Psalm 1:1–3; Galatians 5:22–23.

Drama

Scenes and Wonders (Appendix 2) 'Nearly Ready' (pp 18–20.

Story

'Miss Goodygood Makes Teddy Brown Cross' (Appendix 1.G).

Hymns

'How sweet the name of Jesus sounds'; 'I want to walk with Jesus Christ'; 'Jesus, the very thought of you'; 'Spirit of holiness, wisdom and faithfulness'. Select also from the section of the hymn book on the Holy Spirit.

Prayers

Prayers for all the Family 52; 188; 190; 200; 249; 371; 395.

Main Talk

Preparation

You will need a carpet roll, some cardboard boxes, a pack of balloons, a felt tip pen, a roll of string.

Cut out some simple branch and leaf shapes from the cardboard boxes, and four 'roots'. Paint the carpet roll, the branches and the roots brown, and the leaves green. Staple the leaves to the branches and attach the branches to the carpet roll (making slits and sliding the branches in works well).

Stand the roll and branches wherever you need it and then put the 'roots' on the floor at the base of it. Put a label on the underside of each root which will read 'Prayer', 'Worship', 'Reading the Bible', 'Christian friendship'.

Blow up the balloons and write the fruit of the Spirit on bunches of nine of them. Attach string to one set of nine and tie them loosely around the branches. Hide the spare balloons in an easily accessible place.

Presentation

What is this standing behind me? Notice how healthy it looks. It is like the tree we heard about in Psalm 1. It is thriving. Its leaves are a lovely green and it has plenty of fruit on it. Yet in some parts of Israel (Palestine) such a tree would have stood out. There is so much hot sun and dry wind in that country that lots of trees and shrubs wither and die.

Can you remember what made all the difference to this tree? It was planted near streams of living water. That meant that no matter how much sun there was this tree could still get refreshment and strength. You couldn't see the water—but it was there.

The psalmist says that as believers we should be like

that tree. We should depend on God as the tree depended on the water. So let's think about that.

What does a tree use to drink in water? It uses roots. So what are the equivalent of those roots in our lives as we try to 'drink in' the life of God? Can I have four volunteers— each of you to choose a root and tell me what is written on it. (Each child will pick up a root, read the label and you can comment on each.)

So we have been reminded how God's Spirit comes into our lives, but if that is happening we should expect something else as well. What can you see growing on this tree behind me? Yes, fruit. The water drawn in through the roots leads to the production of fruit. So it should be with us. St Paul says in his letter to the Galatians that we should be able to spot nine fruit of the Spirit in a Christian's life. If I can have nine volunteers, we can choose a fruit and see what they are. (If you want to be quick have scissors to hand to cut the string.) (Talk briefly about each of the fruit.)

So that the rest of you are not disappointed, I have got some more fruit stored away and you can all have one. (Direct them to the hidden balloons.) Now that you all have a balloon remember that it represents the kind of qualities that should be noticeable in your life. But remember you will only be able to produce them if, like the tree in the water, you stay in touch with God. As St Teresa of Avila said, 'Christians should be like trees planted upside down—with their roots in heaven and their fruit on earth.'

Paul Thomas
Upper Poppleton, York

45   The Motorway Services

AIM

To show the importance of having a daily time set apart for God.

TEXT

Matthew 11:25–30.

DRAMA

Drama for all the Family 26 'Climbing'; 37 'Alter Ego'; 59 'The Persistent Widow'. Also *Acting Up* (Appendix 2) 'Praying is Like Breathing', pp 19–20.

STORY

'The Boomerang' (Appendix 1.H).

HYMNS

'Dear Lord and Father of mankind'; 'I heard the voice of Jesus say'; 'Jesus, how lovely you are'; 'Meekness and majesty'; 'O Thou who camest from above'; 'We rest on Thee'; 'What a Friend we have in Jesus'. See also sections in the hymn book on the Bible, the Holy Spirit, and prayer.

PRAYERS

Prayers for all the Family contains a Monthly Cycle of Prayer, with short Bible readings for a year. This might be recommended during the service and prayer 195 used.

MAIN TALK

Preparation

You will need to make four large boards with four road signs from the motorway services. The large P for parking, the fuel pump, the food sign and the bed designating a place to stay overnight. Also make four smaller boards with the words 'Pray', 'Holy Spirit', 'Bible' and 'Rest in God' on them. (Overhead transparencies can work just as well.)

Presentation

Ask the congregation 'Who likes going on holiday?' Point out that the holiday itself is usually great but the travelling there and back can be very tedious (especially if you're a child). Ask 'Who usually goes on their holidays in a car?' 'What is the name of the place where you can stop on the motorway?'

Explain that you've got some signs that you might find at a motorway service station and that you want the congregation to tell you what they mean. Go through each sign, getting a child to come and hold up each sign (if you're using boards).

Explain why it's important for us to stop on long journeys. To give the driver a rest, to refuel the car and to eat.

Go on to say that it is important that we all take time out from our busy lives in order to spend time with God. Tell the congregation that we can compare this to the road signs. There are four things that God says we should do.

First, P stands for prayer. Say how important it is to spend time with God talking to him and listening to him (1 Thess 5:16–18). (Ask a child to hold up the board with Pray on it.)

Secondly the fuel pump shows how we need to ask God to keep on filling us with the Holy Spirit so that we can be powered up to do the things that he wants us to (Acts 1:8). (Ask a child to hold up the board with Holy Spirit on it.)

Thirdly the food sign tells us how we need to continually feed on the word of God, the Bible. Explain how it is God's main way of telling us things and teaching us things (2 Tim 3:16). (Ask a child to hold up the board with Bible on it.)

Finally the bed sign tells us that it's important to rest in God. Say how it is so easy to get wrapped up in all sorts of things so that our lives are so busy we haven't got time to rest in God's love. Comment how very often it is Christians who are involved in Christian work who are the worst for not stopping to rest in God (Mt 11:28–30). (Ask a child to hold up the final board.)

Make a general challenge to everyone as to whether each of us is taking time out from our busy lives to do the above.

Lesley Riley and Philip Sowerbutts
Blackburn

46 Asking—a Talk on Personal Prayer

AIM

To provoke thought about why our prayers sometimes appear not to be answered. (This talk is also suitable for Mothering Sunday).

TEXT

Luke 11:1–13. (See *The Dramatised Bible*, pp 154–5 New Testament section.)

DRAMA

Drama for all the Family 59 'The Persistent Widow'; *Acting Up* (Appendix 2) 'Praying is Like Breathing', pp 19–20.

STORY

In the 1830s George Müller, a man who had great faith in God, was very concerned about all the poor children in Bristol, where he lived, who had no mothers and fathers. He prayed to God about what he should do, and God told him to open up orphan houses for them. The first opened in April 1836.

Because George Müller was so sure this was God's command, he also believed that God would always provide his houses with all they needed, so he never asked publicly for money.

One morning, one of the houses had completely run out of food and money. Müller came in to breakfast, where all the children were standing round the table with totally empty plates and cups in front of them. He raised his hands and prayed, 'Dear Father, we thank you for what you are going to give us to eat.'

At that very moment there was a knock on the door. The baker stood there, and said, 'Mr Müller, I couldn't sleep last night. Somehow I felt you didn't have bread for breakfast, and the Lord wanted me to send you some. So I got up at two o'clock and baked some fresh bread, and have brought it.'

No sooner had George Müller thanked the man, praised God and told the children, when there was a further knock at the door. The local milkman's cart had broken down immediately in front of the orphanage. The milkman wondered if he could give the children the cans of his fresh milk, so that he could empty his wagon and repair it.

Hymns

'Father God in heaven, Lord most high'; 'Lord, teach us how to pray aright'; 'What a Friend we have in Jesus'. See also Prayer section of hymn book.

Prayers

Prayers for all the Family 3; 121 (Litany); 400; 402.

Main Talk

Presentation

Open with series of requests to Mum, eg:

Mum . . . can I have a biscuit?

Mum . . . will you do up my shoelaces?

Mum . . . can I have a pair of trainers like John's got?

Mum . . . can I watch the end of this programme?

All the time, from when we are very, very small, we are always *asking* our mums for things.

When we are very small, we go (make baby squawking noise). What are we asking for? (Elicit answer—food.)

As we grow bigger, we ask for different things:

Mum . . . I'm in the school football team; can you get me a shirt?

Mum . . . can I have £10 please for the school trip?

Mum . . . can I go to Angela's birthday party, and will you collect me at 10.30?

Mum . . . do you think Dad would mind if I asked him to pay for driving lessons?

What is today? (Elicit answer—Mothering Sunday.) This is a day for thinking about our mums and all that they do for us, and how we treat them.

One of the things that we all do to our mums is to ask for things, all the time. Most kind, good mums and dads do what their children ask, but sometimes they don't. Why not? (Elicit answers such as—Not yet; can't do it; can't afford it; not good for you.) We can't always have everything that we ask for, but usually there is a good reason.

The reading from the Bible just now was all about asking for things—asking God our Father in heaven for things. Asking God for things is called praying (though praying means more than just asking).

Jesus' friends and disciples asked him, 'Teach us to pray.' He answered, 'Say this when you pray: "Father . . ."' and he went on to teach them the Lord's Prayer.

In the rest of the reading, Jesus goes on to say that we must keep asking. Trust God to give you what's good for you, just as your mum and dad here do. Always ask—but you may not always get what you ask for. If you don't, it will be because God knows that it wouldn't be good for you.

Michael Grylls
Whitchurch, Hants

47   The Early Church at Prayer

AIM

To encourage the congregation to realise that the early church was just as human as we are when it comes to prayer, but that does not excuse us from faithful praying.

TEXT

Acts 12:1–19.

DRAMA

Show Scripture Union sound-strip or video *On Fire* story 4 'Escape'. Also *Sketches from Scripture* (Appendix 2) 'Pirates', pp 64–66.

HYMNS

Consider William Cowper's 'What various hindrances we meet'; Wallace's 'There is an eye that never sleeps'; and Montgomery's 'Lord, teach us how to pray aright'.

PRAYERS

Prayers for all the Family 202; 402.

Main Talk

Preparation

Prepare the following OHP acetates:

1. Four illustrations as shown in Figure 1, each being placed on the OHP as indicated below. In the case of Peter, have him seated in prison alone, with the guard able to be separately flipped over and the '16 x' also able to be flipped over.

2. See Figure 2. 'Serious' should have only the upper parts of the arms showing, to be joined by the remainder of the bodies when 'corporate' is reached. 'Specific' should be separate, and ready simply to be laid on the OHP.

3. A whole acetate as indicated in Figure 3.

Presentation

Using the criss-cross frame in Figure 1, hold a 'noughts and crosses' quiz on the story of the text, having either used the sound-strip or read the passage (possibly dramatically). The questions could be:

1. Who was Leader of the early Christians?

2. Can you name another important leader mentioned in the story?

3. What happened to him?

4. By whom? (In speaking of Herod's soldiers, put the figure of Herod on the OHP and mention that this Herod's father was the one before whom Jesus came at the time of his trial. His grandfather had had the babies around Bethlehem killed at the time of the first Christmas.)

5. What happened to Peter? (Put him on OHP.)

6. Was he alone? (Add one soldier.) Any more? (Add '16 x'.) Comment that it would seem the Christians must have been seen as very powerful for Herod to take such serious action, namely the deepest part of the prison, probably sixteen soldiers, chains and sentries.

FIGURE 1

FIGURE 2

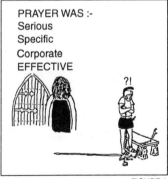

FIGURE 3

People are still put in prison for their faith in Jesus Christ. Some years ago some Christians in Nepal were put in prison, but they were soon released, because they were converting all the other prisoners to Christ!

7. When the church in Jerusalem realised Peter was in prison and probably going to be tortured and killed at the next festival, what did they do? (Put 'praying hands' on OHP.)

8. Name one of the praying group.

9. What happened to Peter?

10. (Reserve question.) How did the Christians behave when first told Peter was at the door?

Clear the OHP.

Let's think a little more about the prayer of that group:

1. *It was serious.* 'Earnestly praying.' (OHP arms in air.) The situation was desperate and there was nothing they could do humanly speaking, but they could pray, and they did.

Their praying is compared to the earnest praying of Jesus in the Garden of Gethsemane, fervent and continuous. It needed to be, because Peter's death was imminent.

How seriously do we take prayer? We recognise the importance of getting out of the way of ambulances and fire-engines to save physical life, but do we have the same concern for those dying spiritually? What effort do we make to pray?

2. *It was specific.* 'For him', that is, for Peter. (OHP.) They named their need very precisely.

Perhaps refer to the parable on prayer in Luke 11:5, where the man is very specific about what he requires from his neighbour, namely 'three loaves'. In our prayers we should name names and needs, not just ask God to bless everybody.

3. *It was corporate.* 'The church was earnestly praying.' (OHP join up arms with bodies.) There is a place for our

private prayers, but Scripture seems to teach that there is special power when we gather together to pray about matters on which we agree.

4. *It was effective.* (Clear the OHP and place third acetate on.) Peter was freed. Let us be encouraged that despite their partial faith God acted.

The God they prayed to is also our God. It is not a question of great faith in God, but faith in a great God.

Summarise the four headings and pray.

Michael Botting
Editor

48 The Lighthouse A Talk on Witness

AIM

To illustrate how Christians should witness to their faith by life and lip.

TEXTS

Matthew 5:16; John 8:12.

DRAMA

Drama for all the Family 40 'Angels'; *Scenes and Wonders* (Appendix 2) 'The Reluctant Evangelist'; *Divine Comedies* (Appendix 2) 'The Great Commission', pp 65–70.

HYMNS

Graham Kendrick's 'Shine, Jesus, shine'.

PRAYERS

Prayers for all the Family see index under 'Witness'.

MAIN TALK

Preparation

Make the following four OHP acetates:
1. A traditional seaside lighthouse.

2. Yellow beams fixed to the above acetate so that they can be flipped across at the appropriate moment to give the impression that the lighthouse is shining

3. The words 'lip' and 'life' in a dark colour that are also attached to the first acetate, and which can be flipped across in turn to land on the beams from the lighthouse.

4. (This is optional and could either fit as part of the first acetate or be completely separate.) Ships seen being guided through dangerous rocks by the aid of the lighthouse beams.

Presentation

Talk about a holiday by the seaside where you have seen a lighthouse. Explain that Christians should be rather like lighthouses. Show your first OHP acetate and ask questions along the following lines:

What is the purpose of a lighthouse? To decorate the seaside? Somewhere for the keeper to live or show people around? You will probably get the answer 'to warn ships of danger', but do not accept that answer to your present question. Only accept the answer 'to give light'. Then ask what people are for? To be amused? To live for themselves? To make a name for themselves? To earn lots of money? Get everyone to turn to Matthew 5:16 and draw out the answer 'to give light'.

How does a lighthouse give light? Does my lighthouse look as if it has light in it? Answer 'No'. Explain that light has to be put in and it has to be in touch with power. But it's dark there now. Are people born with light inside? No. They may look nice on the outside but they are dark inside. Enlarge on sin and our inability to keep God's law. We have to have light brought in. Where do we get the light from? Ask people to look up John 8:12. Explain how we have to receive Jesus, the Light of the World, into our lives, if we are going to be able to shine for him in the world.

Does the lighthouse just keep the light inside so that people can see round and the lighthouse keeper can read his newspaper? Draw out the answer that the lighthouse must shine out. (Flip on the OHP beams.) Ask what else we must do, apart from asking Jesus to be our Saviour. Draw out that we must shine for him. Ask how we do that, and encourage the answer that we must show we are Christians by our life and lip. Flip these OHP acetates on.

Why must a lighthouse shine? So that everyone can see what a wonderful lighthouse it is? No. Draw out 'to warn ships of the danger of rocks and help them find the harbour'. (Put up last OHP acetate.) Why must we shine out? To warn others that they must not live without Jesus Christ, but discover his love and forgiveness and glorify God by their lives lived for him.

Michael Botting
Editor

BIBLICAL CHARACTERS AND
MISCELLANEOUS TALKS

49   God Is!

To show that God is personal, powerful and works to a plan that is good.

TEXT

Genesis 1:6–25.

DRAMA

Drama for all the Family 18 'The Passion', suggested because it begins with the creation, but moves to the crucifixion; *Divine Comedies* (Appendix 2) '98% Proof', pp 106–110.

STORY

'An Old Roman Story' (Appendix 1.U).

HYMNS

'All creatures of our God and King'; 'All people that on earth do dwell'; 'God is working his purpose out'; 'Immortal, invisible, God only wise'; 'Jesus is Lord! creation's voice proclaims it'; 'Thou whose almighty word'.

PRAYERS

Prayers for all the Family 1; 92; 115 (Litany); 124; 125; 207; 335.

MAIN TALK

Preparation

You will need a teazlegraph on which to put up flashcards; a school report form—a blank one will do, but if a completed one is used it could lend itself to an injection of humour, if appropriate; a flower in season, preferably scented; a plan of a house—this could be a proper drawing by an architect or a simple ground plan of any house.

Prepare flashcards with the words: THINK, SPEAK, WORK, PERSON, PERSONAL, POWER, POWERFUL and PLAN.

The words could also be put on acetates and used on an OHP.

Presentation

Do you see what I have in my hand? It's a school report. What sort of things will it tell us? It will tell us what someone is like at school. It will say whether the person works hard and does well or not. It will probably say something about how the person behaves in school and is likely to say whether he or she gets on with the other children and the teachers. A school report gives us a sort of word picture of someone.

Long before school reports were invented, the Bible gave a word picture of God. The things that are written about God in the Bible help us to know what he is like. Let me remind you of the first three words of today's Bible reading: 'And God said . . . ' Now those three words alone tell us a great deal about God. Before a person can say anything, what must happen inside their head? They have to THINK (put up flashcard) of what to say.

So first God thinks, then he begins to SPEAK (flashcard). 'And God said let there be . . . ' So this is where the work begins to happen. God thinks, then he speaks, and the WORK (flashcard) gets done.

Now the Bible tells us that we are made like God—made in his image. That does not mean we look like him. Nobody knows what God looks like. Being made in God's image means he has made us able to do some of the things he does like THINK, SPEAK and WORK. These are abilities God gives to each PERSON (flashcard).

Now just as everyone who reads a school report knows something about the person it is written about, so the Bible tells us not just something about God, but everything we need to know. God wants everyone to read it and to know all about him. This shows he is not some distant being who remains unknown to us. He is a PERSONAL (flashcard) God, who is interested in each person he has made.

(Now produce the flower.) I have brought a bit of God's work with me to church today. As you can see, it's (eg) a rose. A rose is a very lovely part of God's creation. (Here invite a member of the congregation to come and touch the rose and try to describe what it feels like—soft, smooth, silky, delicate or whatever. Somebody else might come and smell the scent and describe that—sweet, fragrant, etc.)

When we look at a delicate rose like this, we do not immediately think of it as something containing great strength or power. Everything about it gives us an idea of gentleness and beauty. Yet it is not something a man can make. Oh yes, he can plant a rose bush and give it all the right conditions for growing well, but that does not always guarantee that roses are going to bud and bloom. If they don't there is nothing anyone can do about it. Only

God has the POWER (flashcard) to give the rose bush the life it needs to produce beautiful roses like this one.

The POWER which God has, to give life, is something we cannot understand. Only God brings things to life by his POWER. It is the same with any other plant. I can put a rather dead looking thing called a seed in the ground. I can give it all the right conditions for growing. But how that dry and dead looking seed receives life is a mystery. Only God is POWERFUL (flashcard) enough to give it life. Our God is POWERFUL.

The last thing I want to show you this morning is a plan of a house. Before a house is built the builder needs a PLAN (flashcard) to follow, so he can get the walls and doors in the right places, and so on. Plans have to be made before anything can be built, if it is to be done properly and not be a disaster. Things like ships, aeroplanes and space rockets, for example, as well as buildings, all need plans to be drawn first. Then everything gets done in the right order.

There are other kinds of plan too. Before going into battle an army general will discuss his plans about how to win the battle. A plan is a very important part of many things that are done in life. As you listened to the Bible reading, did you notice how God was working to a plan? After creating light and darkness and shaping the earth and heaven and sea, God began filling the earth with life— plant life at first, then the creatures in the sea, followed by creatures on land and finally man appeared on the earth. Everything was done to a plan.

Did you notice too how many of the verses in the story ended with the words, 'God saw that it was good'? All the work God did in creation was good. We can usually know what someone is like by the work he does. God's work was good because he planned it that way and he saw that it was good.

Like this beautiful rose here, which is just one example of God's work. God always works to a plan that is good. God has a plan for you and me, so that our lives will be as good as he wants them to be. Let's ask for his POWER to make his PLAN happen in our PERSONAL lives. (Rearrange flashcards on teazlegraph.)

John Bavin
Forden, Welshpool

50 Abraham and the Faithfulness of God

AIM

To teach about Abraham and the faithfulness of God.

TEXTS

Genesis 15:5; Galatians 3:29; Hebrews 11:11–12.

DRAMA

Drama for all the Family 35 'Numbers'.

STORY

Refer back to talk 46 and the story of George Müller, who trusted God's faithfulness. See also 'Except the Lord Build the House . . .' (Appendix 1.W).

HYMNS

'All my hope in God is founded'; 'How firm a foundation, you people of God'; 'My hope is built on nothing less'; 'Rock of ages, cleft for me'; 'The God of Abraham praise'.

PRAYERS

Prayers for all the Family 3; 72; 74; 202; 209; 349.

Main Talk

Preparation

You will need a large jar full of Smarties and a small bottle containing sand. A blackboard or OHP may be helpful, but not essential.

Presentation

Have you ever entered one of those competitions where you have to guess the number of Smarties in a bottle? All you can do is guess, because there's no way you can count them. If you've ever done that, you'll know something of what Abraham must have felt like when, in his late 70s, God took him outside his tent one night and invited him to look up into the starry sky. And God said, 'Your descendants will be as many as those. Think of the sand on the seashore. Your children will be as numerous as that.' We're told that Abraham believed the Lord. I wonder if you would have done if God had said that to you.

At this stage you may wish to enquire how many have been to the seaside recently on holiday. You could then describe where you went (in my case it was Malta), and how you have brought back some sand from the beach there. Hold up a clear glass bottle containing sand. Emphasise how this is just a tiny sample of the vast amount of sand there was on the beach.

Then ask for a volunteer, saying that you need someone of school age who is capable of doing simple arithmetic. When a volunteer comes forward, you could ask them if they are good at addition, and if necessary ask them to demonstrate with a simple sum like 5 + 5 (but be careful not to embarrass them). Then explain that what you would like them to do is to count the grains of sand that there are in your bottle, and that when they've done that, you'll continue with your talk. Hopefully, you should evoke some sort of response indicating that it is impossible, it can't be done. Suggest that you then recruit someone to help them with the counting (I conveniently had a university maths professor in the congregation, but a school-teacher would be almost as good). But the result will be the same. There are too many to count. Ask for a very rough estimate: 5 million? 10 million? Then point out that if there are that many in this little bottle, how many grains of sand are there likely to be on an average-sized beach? Yet this is what God promised Abraham—descendants as many as the sand on the seashore. Outline, in as interesting a way as possible, the essential details of the story of Abraham.

Describe how so many years passed without any sign of a child for Abraham and Sarah. In human terms it looked impossible, because they were so old. But emphasise how the Bible says that you need patience if you are going to receive what God has promised. Illustrate how some people (perhaps some in the congregation) have been praying for years for the conversion of a friend, or a relative, or a marriage partner, and have not yet seen the desired result.

Someone has very rightly said that the biggest fear people have when launching out in faith is what if nothing happens? It's a reasonable question because the nature of faith is to take a line of action before you know how the thing is going to work. Illustrate with a story like someone jumping out of an aeroplane with a parachute, believing that it will work.

But it was nearly a quarter of a century before God's promise to Abraham showed even the first sign of being fulfilled. But it happened, and eventually when Abraham was 100 years old, Isaac was born. He was, if you like, the first grain of sand on the seashore. But what about all the rest? God didn't promise Abraham one descendant, he promised him millions. Has that promise been fulfilled? (Yes.) So who are all the sons and daughters of Abraham that the Bible speaks of? (Us.) Quote Galatians 3:29 (or ask a child to find it and read it out).

Conclude by saying that you want to tell how many sons and daughters of Abraham there are in the world today. It's estimated that in the world today there are 1.8 billion Christians. Write up the 1 and the 8 on an OHP, or blackboard, and invite someone in the congregation to come forward and write the correct number of noughts at the end of these figures. (Bear in mind that there is a disparity between the English billion—a million million—and the American billion—a thousand million. But don't let that become an issue! The point is to convey to the congregation the massive number of Christians in the world today.) Point out that that number doesn't include all the Christians who have ever lived from the time of Abraham. On top of that, across the world, there are sixty new Christians every minute, about 100,000 new Christians every day. Can you see how God fulfils his promises?

We need to have the faith that Abraham had. Romans 4 says that Abraham didn't weaken in faith or waver concerning the promise of God, but he was fully convinced that God was able to do what he had promised. As you go on trusting him and his faithfulness, you will prove in your own experience how faithful he is. He is always able to do what he has promised, whatever your mind or your heart may think or feel.

Tony Ward
Leicester

51   The Call of Moses

AIM

To discover, through the call of Moses, what God is like, what he requires of us and what he promises us.

TEXT

Exodus 3–4.

DRAMA

Drama for all the Family 24 'A Farewell Present'. If this sketch is performed as recommended, with the cast walking from the back of the church to the front, then it is essential that the cast speak up well or have radio microphones.

STORY

The Bible passage is very long and lends itself to dramatic reading as recommended in *The Dramatised Bible* (Appendix 2).

HYMNS

'Be still, for the presence of the Lord' (*Songs of Fellowship* 40); 'We are standing on holy ground' (*Songs of Fellowship* 569); 'The God of Abraham praise' (*Songs of Fellow-*

ship 530, *Hymns for Today's Church* 9); 'Guide me, O my great Redeemer' (*Hymns for Today's Church* 528).

PRAYERS

Prayers for all the Family 4; 213; 398.

MAIN TALK

Preparation

Prepare three OHP acetates as illustrated, with the headings on the base acetates and the various points on acetate material fixed separately with Sellotape to the left-hand edge of the base acetates, so that they can be flipped over into view at the appropriate moment.

Presentation

Begin by saying that we are going to consider how God spoke to Moses, but there is no point in having a sermon unless we also believe God still speaks today. Let's ask him to do so this morning. (Lead in suitable prayer.)

Refer to a head of the London Bible College who was once asked a very important question by a small and very serious boy of eight.

WHAT IS GOD LIKE? (OHP)

Something we all want to know. This story of Moses helps us to find out. Briefly tell the story of Moses thus far. Then when out tending sheep he sees a burning bush. He did not need to be a scientist to know that when fire comes from a bush it normally burns up! He investigates.

God speaks to him and he, and we, learn the first fact about God.

1. **Holy** (OHP)

'Moses! . . . Take off your sandals, for the place where you are standing is holy ground.'

God is perfect, Moses and all of us are sinful. We often do wrong things. We're unholy.

2. **Eternal** (OHP)

God tells Moses he is the God of his forefathers—Abraham, Isaac and Jacob (later renamed Israel). Some verses later God tells Moses the special name by which he is to be known 'I Am Who I Am'. Very strange—but it suggests he is eternal, the ever present one. We can't understand it, but God has always existed and always will. He's not only got the whole world in his hands, but the whole universe and the whole of history. So he is just as present with us here in (name your church) now as he was with Moses those thousands of years ago.

3. **Loving** (OHP)

God went on to explain that he knew all about the suffering of the Children of Israel in Egypt and was planning to do something about it that would eventually bring them into a wonderful country—Canaan, 'flowing with milk and honey'.

God knows all about our problems, too. The big problems like (name, say, N. Ireland), and the smaller ones of our everyday lives. In his love he longs to do something about them, but . . .

4. **Demanding** (OHP)

God works his plans through people. That's why he was calling Moses. 'So now, go. I am sending you to Pharaoh to bring my people the Israelites out of Egypt' (3:10). Note there was no 'by your leave', Moses was told to GO. Which brings us to a second question.

WHAT DOES GOD ASK OF US? (OHP)

1. **Humility** (OHP)

Moses had to humble himself when he came before God,

taking off his shoes. When we come to God we do not literally have to do that, but we do have to tell God we are sorry for our sins, which can be very humbling, because we are all naturally proud.

2. Faith (OHP)

Moses was concerned that when he came to the Children of Israel they would not believe that the Lord had sent him. So the Lord says he will give various signs to show Moses had come from him.

Refer to the staff becoming a snake, Moses' hand becoming leprous, the Nile becoming like blood (the first of the plagues of Egypt).

God cannot act for us unless we have faith. Faith is more than just believing something with our heads, it means trusting with our hearts. Hence, 'Do you believe and trust?' in baptism and confirmation services. Refer to couples' promises in the marriage service.

3. Obedience (OHP)

Moses made several excuses as to why he should not obey God's demands, eventually saying, 'O Lord, please send someone else to do it' (4:13).

At this point God got cross with him. God was telling him to leave his sheep and go to Pharaoh. He expected to be obeyed. Has God been speaking to you on some matter and you are hesitating? He expects, indeed demands, obedience.

However, we come to our third and last question.

WHAT DOES GOD PROMISE US? (OHP)

God understood Moses' problems. He was not going to leave him on his own. God made three special promises:

1. His presence (OHP)

When he first called Moses he said, 'I will be with you' (3:12).

2. His power (OHP)

The miraculous signs and the plagues, ending with slaying of the first born.

3. His provision (OHP)

One of the excuses Moses put to God was that he was no speaker. He had no gift with words. God asked him, 'Who gave man his mouth? . . . Is it not I, the Lord?' (4:11). Then came the promise: 'Now go; I will help you speak and will teach you what to say' (4:12). Further, God reminded him that he had a brother, Aaron.

Read 4:14–16. Two mouths to speak.

> 3:21–22 God would even make the Egyptians make a back payment of Israelite wages!

So Moses eventually obeyed, leading to the Passover, the Exodus, Mount Sinai and the Promised Land.

Conclusion

All this happened so many years ago, but God has not changed because, as we have seen, he is eternal. What we have been thinking about concerning Moses has application to us too.

When Jesus spoke to his disciples, before he left them, he told them they were to be his witnesses, which meant opening their mouths for the Lord. He made similar promises to them that God made to Moses.

(The Drama suggested above could start at this moment.)

God promises us:

His presence—to the end of the age through his Holy Spirit.

His power—the Holy Spirit himself in all his fullness.

His provision—especially his gifts to witness.

And he has called us to be his witnesses now!

Michael Botting
Editor

52 Josiah and Tyndale

AIM

Using the story of King Josiah and some original drama material about Bible translator William Tyndale to encourage us to value, read and obey the Bible. Especially suitable for Bible Sunday (Advent 2 or 3rd before Christmas).

TEXTS

2 Kings 22:1–23, 30; 2 Chronicles 34–35.

DRAMA

William Tyndale (Appendix 1.Y).

STORY

'The Influence of the Bible' (Appendix 1.V).

HYMNS

'How firm a foundation, you people of God'; Christopher Idle's hymn 'How sure the Scriptures are', (*Hymns for Today's Church* 249).

PRAYERS

ASB 1980, p 426, Collect appointed for 2nd Sunday in Advent, p 844, Collect appointed for a Martyr. See also Index of *Prayers for all the Family* under Bible.

MAIN TALK

Preparation

Prepare four OHP acetates as follows:

1. A school blackboard on an easle, with the words: Reading, Riting, Rithmetic able to be flipped on or off the board.

Words: Reformation, Revelation, Redemption, able to be flipped on or off blackboard.

2. REFORMATION: people worshipping pagan idols. Also make to flip over, people worshipping modern idols, money, TV, etc.

3. REVELATION: king being shown scroll. And to flip over, a modern Bible, say *Good News*.

4. REDEMPTION: simple illustration of a door with the sideposts and lintel being splashed with blood. And to flip over, Jesus holding patten and chalice, and Jesus on the cross.

Presentation

Ask if anyone present is eight years old.

Explain that we are going to think about a boy of that age who became King of Judah and lived in that part of the world we now call Israel. He was Josiah, related to King David and King Solomon, who lived many years before him.

There are several ways in which his life and times were similar to those of William Tyndale and they also have a message for us.

Who knows what the three Rs are that we learn at school? (Show OHP acetate 1.) We are going to think of three other Rs, which are rather longer.

1. REFORMATION

When Josiah became a teenager of sixteen he began to seek after God, and by the time he was twenty he was very concerned about the wicked things going on in his kingdom; things like the worshipping of idols (OHP acetate). He had these idols destroyed, which meant that he was trying to reform his people's religion (2 Chron 34:3–7).

In England, when Tyndale was brought up, there was idolatry mixed with religion; things such as the bones of saints and the bread and wine used in the Holy Communion service. As we heard in the drama, Tyndale was told to study the heathen religion for eight or nine years. Like Judah, England needed reformation too.

But we can also make idols of things like money (the National Lottery), or possessions like TV, cars, etc (OHP acetate). Perhaps there should be a reformation or change in our lives.

2. REVELATION

When Josiah was twenty-six the temple in Jerusalem was being repaired, because it had been allowed by earlier kings to fall into ruin. While this was going on, one of the priests of the temple found the Book of the Law— probably part of Deuteronomy, an earlier part of the Bible (OHP acetate). King Josiah was shown this and he realised that a lot of what God said in this book was not being obeyed. God had revealed his laws through this book. Quote 2 Kings 23:24.

Tyndale also had discovered God revealed himself, or spoke to him, through the Bible and he worked hard at his translation of it into simple English, so that even the simplest people could understand it.

Today many people are being helped to understand the Bible because of simpler translations or paraphrases, like *Letters to Young Churches* by J.B. Phillips, or more recently the *Good News Bible* from the Bible Society (OHP acetate). Perhaps we need to read these simpler versions so that God may reveal himself to us.

3. REDEMPTION

The most important revelation to Josiah was that God had made a covenant with his people. Long before God gave the people the Law he had made them his special people. Compare with joining a club, becoming a Scout or Guide or getting married, which involve making a kind of covenant. God especially showed this when he delivered his people out of Egypt, where they had been slaves.

On the night that they left they were told to celebrate the Passover (OHP acetate and explain). Josiah now celebrated the Passover—something which had not happened since the days of Samuel. One of the great prophets of Judah at the time of Josiah was Jeremiah, who prophesied that future generations would come to know God in a very special way. Quote Jeremiah 31:31–34.

The prayer that Tyndale cried from the stake—'Lord, open the King of England's eyes!'—was wonderfully answered only three years later, when the Great Bible was ordered to be provided and placed in all the parish churches of England.

So as a result of Tyndale's translation readers could discover that Jesus is the true Lamb of God, who had died on the cross for their sins (OHP acetate). If they received him as their Saviour they could know they had been redeemed from the consequences of their sins.

Every time the service of the Lord's Supper or Holy Communion was celebrated, it would remind them of their redemption from sin.

That same message is for us too, but we can now have Bibles of our own, and can read them for ourselves.

The Bible says that 'neither before nor after Josiah was there a king like him who turned to the Lord as he did—with all his heart and with all his soul and with all his strength. . . ' (2 Kings 23:25).

Tyndale's work of translation has been so valuable that

our Bibles today are based on it, and he is remembered
500 years after his birth with thanksgiving.

How are our lives going to be remembered?

Michael Botting
Editor

53   The Psalms

Aims

To discover that although the writers of the Psalms sometimes failed to see God in their lives, he was always with
them.

Text

The talk is not based on one particular Psalm, but it would
be appropriate to read say, 78:1–8, 95 or part of 139.

Drama

Drama for all the Family 18 'The Passion', and 19
'Nailed' (Psalm 22 is quoted in both).

Story

There is a story told of a young Scots boy who greatly
enjoyed spending time with the sheep in the Scottish
Highlands. He was befriended by an elderly shepherd,
who was a Christian. In the course of their talks together
while tending the sheep, the older man told the laddie of
the Good Shepherd, and he taught him Psalm 23. He got
the lad to spell out the first line of the Psalm on his thumb
and fingers—'The Lord is my Shepherd', one finger for
each word, hoping that one day the boy would come to

225

know the Good Shepherd, the Lord Jesus, for himself (Jn 10:11).

One day there was a very severe snow storm on the hills where the pair normally watched the flocks, and they got separated. The shepherd reached safety, but the boy was lost for several days. Eventually he was located, very sadly dead through extreme exposure. The shepherd was comforted, however, to note that when his young friend died he was firmly holding the fourth finger of his left hand—'The Lord is *my* Shepherd'.

HYMNS

Use hymns directly based on Psalms, like 'Praise, my soul, the King of heaven' (103), 'The Lord's my Shepherd' (23), etc.

PRAYERS

Bible Praying (Appendix 2) 82 (Confession based on Psalm 119:1–8), 201 (Creed based on Psalm 145).

MAIN TALK

Preparation

Figure 1 shows the final appearance of the OHP acetate which forms the basis of the talk. It is prepared as follows:

- The letters P S A L M are written on the main acetate as shown.
- The five word-endings (raise, ongs, etc) are written on separate pieces of acetate, each of which is hinged to the right edge of the main acetate alongside the corresponding letter.
- The five pictures are each drawn on a small square of

acetate, to be laid on the main acetate as the talk progresses.

Figure 2 shows the shapes (in black) of seven pieces of paper which are required for the second part of the talk.

Presentation

Perhaps begin with Martin Luther's comment that the Psalms are like a garden, the beauty of which lies in the variety of shapes and colours and fragrances.

Place picture (a) on the acetate as shown. The Psalms were written not just to be said but to be sung, and we still sing them today in different forms. Psalms are *Songs*—lift over the flap showing 'ongs'.

Place picture (b). Psalms are special kinds of songs; like the title of the TV programme, they are songs of *Praise*—lift over 'raise'.

Place picture (c). The writers praised God as King of all creation, for his greatness, power and glory. They praised him for his *Majesty*—lift over 'ajesty'.

Place picture (d). As well as praising God for who he is and what he is like, they praised him for what he had done for them—especially for leading them out of Egypt through the Red Sea (Ps 78 and 106). They praised him for his *Acts*—lift over 'cts'.

Place picture (e). But the writers were sometimes sad too, for it seemed God let other people get away with evil and he did not help his own people. So they cried out to God for help. The Psalms are *Laments*—lift over 'aments'.

God may seem distant from us too at times; we may feel angry with God, or sad, or confused. Reading the Psalms helps us to see others have felt that way too; helps us to cope with our feelings; and encourages us to tell God about our feelings and to ask for his help.

But God is always with his people, whether or not we

FIGURE 1

(b) **P**raise

(a) **S**ongs

(d) **A**cts

(e) **L**aments

(c) **M**ajesty

FIGURE 2

FIGURE 3

feel him near, whether or not we can see him at work in our lives. This can be understood better with the help of some 'code', as follows.

Remove the first acetate and place the seven cut-out shapes on the OHP as shown, placing each one quite deliberately and slowly. (As these shapes are easily confused, and as it is important to get the spacing between them correct, it is wise to have a copy of the completed 'code' nearby to check against!) If time allows, place each piece when a question about the Psalms has been correctly answered, eg Who wrote most of them? How many are there?

As we look, the word JESUS can sometimes be seen, and at other times we look hard but it seems hidden. (Some people may find it hard to see the word JESUS; they may find it easier if a strip of lightly coloured acetate, as shown by the shading in Figure 3, is laid across the whole length of the 'code'. Alternately replacing it and removing it adds to the effect of Jesus being seen and then not seen.) God sent his Son Jesus so that we could see what God is like and understand how he loves us; but sometimes it is hard to feel Jesus near to us, and hard to see his loving activity in our lives—just as the psalmists found it hard to believe God was still with them. But he was—and he is!

The Psalms help us to express to God our anger and frustrations, as well as our love and joy, and to ask for his help in our lives. Like the writers of the Psalms, we can discover that being honest with God leads to true praise of him and deeper trust in him.

Brian Fortnum
Speldhurst, Tunbridge Wells

54   The Validity of Jesus' Testimony

Aɪᴍ

To show that the claims of Jesus were upheld by God the Father himself.

Tᴇxᴛs

Mark 1:9–12; Luke 3:15–22.

Dʀᴀᴍᴀ

Drama for all the Family 53 'A Quick Transformation'; 32 'The Right Credentials'.

Sᴛᴏʀʏ

'It is True' (Appendix 1.X).

Hʏᴍɴs

'At the name of Jesus'; 'Be still, for the presence of the Lord'; 'Come let us join our cheerful songs'; 'Jesus, the name high over all'; 'Spirit of the living God'.

Pʀᴀʏᴇʀs

Prayers for all the Family 18, 33, 207, 215.

MAIN TALK

Preparation

You will need a passport—either a full British Passport or the newer EC one.

Stick a sheet of blue card to a sheet of white card and fold down the middle to make a large 'passport'. On the front cover use gold or silver paper to make the lettering 'HEAVEN'S PASSPORT OFFICE'. Decorate with a crown or trumpets.

On the inside front page write 'This is to certify that the holder of this passport is my son. Signed: GOD.'

On the third side draw a 'passport photo' of Jesus with the words underneath 'BEARER: GOD'S SON'.

Presentation

Hold up the real passport and ask the congregation if they know what it is and what it is used for.

Explain that when you go to another country it is not good enough to say who you are. Some proof is required. That is why we have passports.

In order to get my passport I had to send off my birth certificate to a government office. There someone checked that I am who I say I am. So at a foreign border it is the government's word that is accepted.

Listen to what my passport says: 'Her Britannic Majesty's Principal Secretary of State . . . etc' (or EC passport version).

Show the cardboard passport. If Jesus had had a passport I think it would have looked something like this. It would need to be signed by someone who could prove the identity of Jesus. King Herod in Jerusalem wouldn't have been good enough nor would the Emperor in Rome. It had to be God himself.

Jesus didn't have a passport, but there were occasions

when God validated Jesus' testimony. At Jesus' baptism (Mk 1:11) a voice came from heaven: 'You are my Son.' And at the transfiguration (Mk 9:7) 'This is my Son.' But the biggest proof of all is the resurrection of Jesus. God raised his Son from death and burial to new life (Acts 2: 31–32). When the Pharisees challenged Jesus for proof of who he was he reminded them of their own law which stated that the testimony of two men is valid. 'I am the one who testifies for myself, my other witness is the Father who sent me' (Jn 8:17). Jesus then goes on to say that the proof of his identity they desired would be made known when he was lifted up, a reference to his death (Jn 8:27–28).

I am believed that I am who I say I am because a higher authority validates my claim. Why do we believe that Jesus is God's Son? We can believe because we have it on the authority of God himself expressed by God's words and actions.

David Titley
Bloxwich

55 The Puzzle of the Face of Jesus

AIM

To show that the purpose of the members of the church is to work together in unity to reveal Jesus to the world.

TEXT

1 Corinthians 12:12–26.

DRAMA

Drama for all the Family 38 'Bodywork'; 39 'The Cake'. See also, *Divine Comedies* (Appendix 2) 'Body Language pp 102–105, but note Nigel Forde's comments on p 101.

HYMNS

'Bind us together, Lord'; 'Christ, from whom all blessings flow'; 'Make us one, Lord'; 'Spirit of the living God, move among us all'; 'The church's one foundation'.

PRAYERS

Prayers for all the Family 147; 148; 156; 211; 250.

MAIN TALK

Preparation

Visual aid: A picture of the face of Jesus with crown of thorns, cut up to make a jigsaw puzzle. Pieces of Velcro on both sides so that the pieces can be stuck to a Teazlegraph board either way up.

Presentation

1. Take a piece of the puzzle and say that most of us find ourselves to be a bit of a puzzle; it's difficult to understand ourselves, and certainly others find us confusing and puzzling. The parts of the piece that curve outwards are our strengths and the inward curves represent our weaknesses. Our weaknesses are an important part of us. The shape of the piece suggests that we need other pieces.

2. Place other pieces on the board, with the picture side of the puzzle against the board. Write the names of various people in the congregation on the pieces of the puzzle, including the minister. Explain that each piece of the puzzle is different because each of us is different.

3. Ask people what has to be done next in order to do the puzzle. Usually people say 'Start at the corners,' but in fact the first thing is that the pieces have to be turned over. Turn one of the pieces over, and reveal that there is a picture on the other side. Point out that we have to be turned over in order that the picture of which we are part may be revealed. We notice that when the piece is turned over, the name is not visible any longer. We all need to ask ourselves whether we have allowed God to turn us over. Unless we have been turned over we cannot be the people God wants us to be.

4. Turn over all the pieces and link two of them together, explaining that as we show love and understanding to one another we come together in love. Gradually put all the pieces together until the face of Jesus Christ is revealed, and explain that in each one of us who belongs to Jesus, something of him is revealed, but it is only when we show love and concern for one another that the face of Jesus is revealed in such a way that those in the community can see him. Some of us are like an eye who see for him; others are like an ear who hear for him; others are like the crown of thorns because we suffer for him. Ask if anyone can remember which name was on which piece of the puzzle. When we are relating properly to one another and allowing the face of Jesus to be seen in the church, then our own position and importance do not matter; even the minister does not stand out!

5. When the puzzle is completed, there can be one piece missing. You can try and add that piece into the puzzle the wrong way up and show that often people try to do this, but it won't work. The piece has to be turned over as well in order to become part of the puzzle.

6. An addition which I sometimes use: I try and link together one piece that has been turned over and one piece that hasn't been turned over, and say that the two pieces will never join properly. This is what happens when somebody who is a Christian and somebody who is not a Christian marry. (I was using this visual aid with an adult congregation and just referred to this in passing, and I heard afterwards from the minister of the church that God had used the illustration to help somebody review the relationship in which he was getting involved.)

7. Another addition: When we cause division in the church, we tear apart the face of Christ. Do we realise

what we are doing by our words and actions? (When I tore apart the picture of the face at a parish weekend conference some of the adults present were moved to tears.)

There are many messages in this puzzle, not all of them should be used at once. It is just as effective with adult congregations as with all ages present. I have also used this idea with acetates on an OHP, but it is not nearly so effective.

Peter Markby
Southover, Lewes

56 The Call of Peter (Also Suitable for Sea Sunday)

Aɪᴍ

To teach that the best way to run our lives is with Jesus in charge.

Tᴇxᴛ

Luke 5:1–11.

Dʀᴀᴍᴀ

See *The Dramatised Bible* (Appendix 2) p 131, New Testament section.

Sᴛᴏʀʏ

'The Tape Measure' (Appendix 1.J).

Hʏᴍɴs

'Dear Lord and Father of mankind'; 'I want to walk with Jesus Christ'; 'I will make you fishers of men'; 'Jesus calls us! - o'er the tumult'.

Pʀᴀʏᴇʀs

Prayers for all the Family 28; 188; 300; 399; 405.

Main Talk

Preparation

Gather a collection of assorted toy and model boats.

Presentation

1. Give out all the boats, starting with the children and working up to the adults if you have enough boats! Talk a little bit about all the different kinds of boats—what makes them go, etc. Move on to talk about the different kinds of skills needed to get the different boats to go where we might want them to (expand on this for a Sea Sunday service). In all these different skills, how many of us would think that God and prayer might be essential?

2. Most people, even if they believe in God, don't see him as necessary for the practical things of their daily work. We tend to think of God as being there to help us when we can't manage, and we don't give him a second thought when we come to things we can manage and are good at by ourselves. Peter, as we see him in Luke 5, must have been a bit like that.

3. Peter, brought up a Jew, believed in God, and must certainly have respected God. When 'something religious' was happening (ie Jesus coming along to preach), he was happy to lend out his boat as a pulpit and let those who were 'religious' get on with it. When it came to fishing, however, Peter knew what was what; he was good at it and he was definitely in charge.

4. That was the point at which Jesus challenged him. Peter quickly saw that he, the master fisherman, had been bettered by the wandering Preacher. Even at fishing, Jesus knew best, and when Peter obeyed he had his best catch ever.

5. Through it all, Peter learned:
   (a) He was wrong to doubt Jesus (verse 8).
   (b) He was right to trust and obey Jesus.
   (c) Jesus had a job for him that would use his skills for God's work.
   (d) The best way to live is to let Jesus take charge and not to hold anything back.

Robert Simpson
Shirwell, Barnstable

57   Thomas—Man of Faith

Aɪᴍ

To show that belief begins when we take a step of faith, of which Thomas proved to be a remarkable example.

Tᴇxᴛ

John 20:19–29, which could be dramatised (see *The Dramatised Bible* pp 243–4 New Testament section).

Dʀᴀᴍᴀ

Drama for all the Family 23 'I'll Soon Wipe That Scowl off Tommy's Face'.

Sᴛᴏʀʏ

Many years ago a bridge had to be built across a deep canyon in the United States of America, before all the modern equipment was available that is taken for granted today. Those responsible for the bridge built it on one side on rollers. Then workmen assembled on both sides of the canyon where the bridge was required and a heavy object, which had string attached to it, was thrown across the canyon. The object was removed and stronger string tied to the initial string, which was pulled back across the canyon. To that string was tied rope; to the rope—wire;

240

to the wire—chain. Eventually the bridge was pulled across till the sides of the canyon were joined.

Faith is like that. There has to be that initial 'throw' to make contact. Then follows the growth of faith, getting stronger and stronger as the Christian life proceeds.

HYMNS

'From heaven you came'; 'Jesus stand among us'. See also section in the hymn book on the resurrection and faith.

PRAYERS

Prayers for all the Family 46; 54; 72; 74; 202.

MAIN TALK

Preparation

Prepare three large cards: one with an eye on, one with an ear on, and one with a hand on.

Also prepare cards with the words 'STOP DOUBTING AND BELIEVE' all chopped up into half-words and letters. These will be re-assembled in the talk.

Presentation

NOTE: The Bible never tells us that Thomas doubted, but that he did not believe. Earlier translations of John 20:27 use the word 'faithless', modern versions 'doubt', and doubting is normally attributed to this apostle, so Editor and Author accept this.

If ever there was a man who has been misunderstood it is the apostle Thomas. Tell a story about a misunderstanding.

A dustman was on his rounds and he was outside a

house and just couldn't find the bin. So he stood at the door and rang the bell.

'Where's yer bin, mate?' he said.

'Oh, I bin to Hong Kong,' came the reply.

'No, where's yer bin?' said the dustman.

'I bin to Hong Kong.'

'Where's yer *wheely* bin, mate?' said the dustman.

'I weely, weely bin to Hong Kong!'

Poor old Thomas—he's always known as what? (Doubting Thomas.) It's so sad because he may have had his doubts, yet the last words we hear him say to Jesus are 'My Lord and my God.' Words of faith.

After all we don't refer to the apostle Paul as 'Persecuting Paul', do we? And yet he did persecute the first Christians. And we don't call the apostle Matthew 'Miserly Matthew', yet before he was a believer he was a crooked tax-collector.

Poor Thomas! Explain you will spend a few minutes this morning discovering a little more about this man Thomas and about his faith (*not* his doubts) and see if we can learn anything about ourselves in the process.

Thomas must have wanted to believe. He was part of the inner group of Jesus' disciples and was with them after Jesus had risen from the dead. But for some reason he was not with them when Jesus first appeared to the disciples.

I bet he really wanted to believe that Jesus could come back to life. Then imagine how he felt when he found that all the others except him had actually seen Jesus. He *heard* (get a volunteer to lift up the 'ear' card) from them how they had seen him and how they knew that Jesus really was God and really had risen, just as he said he would.

But hearing it from others just wasn't enough for Thomas. In fact even if he *saw* Jesus himself that wouldn't be enough, he said. (Get a volunteer to lift up the 'eye' card.) Perhaps he thought his eyes would deceive him. What Thomas needed was hard proof—not just hearsay or even sight, but experience—to *touch* Jesus; that's what would be needed for Thomas to believe. (Get a volunteer to lift up the 'hand' card.)

Thomas was a man searching for the truth about Jesus. He truly wanted to have faith, but something inside stopped him from taking that step of faith. Actually it wasn't a very big step, because he had heard and he was willing to listen. But he was a man who was *really confused* about Jesus and about who he really was.

Explain you have brought an anagram, which is a word which is all mixed up and needs sorting out. Ask for a volunteer to have a go. (The answer is: 'Stop doubting—and believe' [verse 27].)

These are words for people today. Often we meet people who say that they want to believe in Jesus and yet something is stopping them.

A recent quote in a newspaper read: 'Belief in God is fairly general, yet those who *know* him seem to be few.'

Perhaps there are some here who would like to believe, but something is stopping you. It might be that you can't understand why God allows suffering in the world, or you can't quite believe that miracles happened, or maybe it's the church that stops you taking that step of faith.

Perhaps you've *heard* about Jesus and know a little of his life story. Maybe you've *seen* a little how he has changed other people's lives but, like Thomas, you need to *touch* him, to experience him in your own life before you'll really believe.

What will it take for you to believe? Whatever it is I want to say to you the words that Jesus said to Thomas; words that turned a doubter into a believer: 'Stop doubting and believe.'

Faith is a wonderful gift from God. It may only start very small. Do you know how to walk from John O'Groats to Land's End? One step at a time. Every journey starts with just one step.

To Jesus' offer of friendship and faith Thomas answered, 'My Lord and my God.' In other words, 'I believe and trust in you.' (Words used in the Baptism service.)

Tradition has it that Thomas went on to be a missionary to India and it was he who first brought the gospel to that country. See how God used him when he was willing to put his life in God's hands and to trust him. To take a small step of faith on a long journey with God.

To all of you here God says, 'Stop doubting and believe.' It will change your life as it changed Thomas' and has changed millions of others after him.

Peter Hall
Bromyard, Herefordshire

58 Peter, John and a Lame Man

To show that, by the way we live, we can show forth Jesus.

T<small>EXTS</small>

Acts 4:13—'Observing that Peter and John were uneducated laymen, they were astonished at their boldness and took note that they had been companions of Jesus' (REB). Also Acts 3:1–16.

D<small>RAMA</small>

There is drama in the talk. However, as a way of illustrating the story, the Scripture Union sound-strip or video *On Fire* part 2 'Bag of Bones' could be shown.

S<small>TORY</small>

At a certain factory there was at least one man who was a committed Christian. He was greatly respected for his high standard of behaviour and the general conduct of his life. One day a fellow worker approached him to say that he had very recently become a Christian. 'That's tremendous,' said the man. 'That makes at least two of us in the place.' 'You a Christian!' said the other man. 'For heaven's sake why did you never tell anyone? For ages

245

I have put off becoming one, because I argued that if it was possible to live the sort of life you live, without being a Christian, why should I bother? Your very silence has delayed my coming to faith.'

HYMNS

'Be bold, be strong, for the Lord our God is with you'; 'Fill now my life, O Lord my God'; 'Forth in the peace of Christ we go'; 'Jesus bids us shine'; 'Jesus' love is very wonderful'; 'Lord, speak to me that I may speak'; 'Shine, Jesus, shine'; 'Tell out my soul'.

PRAYERS

Prayers for all the Family Witness: 5, 51, 52, 65, 149, 196; the sick: 176–181.

MAIN TALK

Preparation

There is some acting involved in this presentation, and it will succeed better if those chosen to act have had some rehearsal. The actions could take place without speaking as the story is being told or read, but if you have competent actors, they might like to speak (or read) their own words. Not much dressing up is needed—the characters can wear towelling gowns and a piece of material for head gear, held on by a head band. The lame man will need some sort of begging bowl, preferably wooden.

It is suggested that children take the parts of Peter, John and the lame man, with other children (as many as you have space for) being the people going in and out of the temple and watching what happens when the lame man is healed.

For the second part (Acts 4—Peter and John in prison and before the court), it might be better if adults took the parts in order to bring them in to an active share in the service.

Presentation

1. One day, at about 3 o'clock, Jesus' friends Peter and John went to the temple to pray—as they often did. All sorts of people were going in and out, people in brightly-coloured robes, mothers and fathers, older people and children. There was a lovely gate called the Beautiful Gate, which had steps leading up to it, and this was the gate which Peter and John went through.

There was one man who was a cripple who had never been able to walk all his life. His friends used to carry him to the temple each day and sit him on the steps so that he could beg for money.

When the lame man saw Peter and John coming up the steps, perhaps he thought they looked kind and would be sure to give him something; so he looked hard at them and held out his bowl.

Peter said to the man, 'Look at us. I have no silver or gold, but what I have I give you: *in the name of Jesus Christ of Nazareth, rise up and walk*' (to be said slowly and emphatically).

Peter grasped him by the right hand and helped him up. At once the man's feet and ankles grew strong and he sprang up and started to walk! He leapt up for the first time in his life and went with Peter and John into the temple, jumping about and praising God as he went. All the people around were amazed! Could this really be the man who had never walked? It was!

Peter saw the people looking and said, 'Why are you

staring at us as if *we* had made this man walk by our own power? No, it was all done by God's power in Jesus' name.' And he continued to tell the people about how Jesus had been crucified because of their sins, but how God had raised him from the dead.

Break for hymn, reading (Acts 3:1–16), and prayers for the sick.

2. Now there were some people who didn't think it at all wonderful. They were very annoyed with Peter and John for telling the people about Jesus. They arrested Peter and John and had them put in prison for the night.

Next day they were brought before the Council. (Semi-circle of Council members with Peter and John and the lame man in the centre, facing them.)

'By what power or by what name did you heal the lame man?' the Council asked.

'It was in the name of Jesus Christ of Nazareth,' said Peter. 'Through him this man was made well. Jesus is the only one who can save us from our sins.'

The members of the Council were amazed that ordinary men, fishermen like Peter and John, could be so bold and could speak so well, because they weren't very clever or well-educated. Then the Council remembered something: *these men had been friends of Jesus*! (All repeat Acts 4:13 together.) Can people say this about us? Can they tell that we are friends of Jesus by the things we do and say?

The Council discussed it among themselves but didn't know what to do about it. The man was obviously healed, and was standing there fit and well—so they couldn't say that Peter and John had not been the means of this miracle. In the end they told Peter and John to go outside while they discussed it.

'We must stop this spreading any further,' they said.

'We'll have to tell them not to go on talking about Jesus as they have been doing.'

So they called them back. 'You are never again to speak or teach about Jesus,' they said. Peter wasn't having this! 'Is it right to obey you or to obey God?' he replied. 'We cannot stop speaking about what we have seen and heard.'

The Council continued to caution them and then let them go—for all the people were praising God for what had happened.

Peter and John went back to their friends and they all prayed to God asking him to make them bold (verse 29).

Discussion

If possible break into small groups of adults and children together, and discuss the following for a few minutes:

(a) What opportunities do we have today for telling people about Jesus?

(b) What would you do if someone told you never to speak about Jesus again?

Finish with a prayer asking God to help us to be bold when we have a chance to talk to someone about Jesus.

P. J. Hunt
Knutsford

59   Philip and the Ethiopian Treasurer

AIM

To tell the story of Philip the Evangelist's encounter with the Ethiopian treasurer and the subsequent baptism. This talk is particularly suitable for an Anglican Baptism service, but can be adapted for other denominations.

TEXT

Acts 8:26–40 (this need not be read if the sound-strip is shown). If it is read a dramatised version can be found in *The Dramatised Bible* (Appendix 2).

DRAMA

Show the Scripture Union sound-strip or video *On Fire* part 3 'The Riddle'. Also *Divine Comedies* (Appendix 2) 'The Hitchhiker's Guide to the Gospel', pp 23–32.

STORY

This might be an occasion for a brief testimony from someone who has had a quite specific conversion to faith in Jesus Christ. However it should be mentioned that for many people the experience is much more likely to be gradual.

H<small>YMNS</small>

'Lord, speak to me that I may speak' (*Hymns for Today's Church* 510). See also in the Scripture and Baptism sections of the hymn book.

P<small>RAYERS</small>

Church Family Worship (Appendix 2) Section 6 'At a Baptism'; ASB Baptism Service.

M<small>AIN</small> T<small>ALK</small>

Preparation

Attach to an OHP acetate twelve small pictures as illustrated. The presentation below should make clear exactly what the pictures are intended to represent.

The four at the top and the four at the bottom can be fixed to the top and bottom edges. The four in the middle are fixed so that 'Sin' and 'The Bible' are both fixed to the left side, the latter extending over the former. The church interior and the cross are fixed to the right, the former having a blank space to the right that is covered by the latter eventually.

Presentation

1. *The child and the chemist*

Show the top left-hand picture. Ask what might be wrong with the child. Suppose it is a tummy ache, what might his or her mother do? Explain about seeing the doctor (2), handing over prescription and purchasing medicine at chemist (3), taking medicine and feeling better (4).

2. *Our spiritual sickness and cure*

We are all sinners and need to take trouble about a cure, as we would a bad tummy ache (Rom 3:23; 6:23). (Show 5.)

Ask where the Ethiopian eventually found a solution to his problem (6). Who helped him to understand it? Philip, who represented the church (7). Did he eat the scroll of Isaiah? No. No more than the child ate the paper the prescription was written on. But just as the prescription led to the medicine, so the Bible passage led to Jesus and what he did for the Ethiopian and us on the cross (8). Explain Isaiah 53 and the need to believe.

3. *Baptism and faith*

Small babies have obviously not sinned, but it soon becomes clear they are born sinners and show it (9). They need to be brought up in a family that reads the Bible and prays (10). They should be brought to church, where they will be helped to understand the Bible and come to faith in Jesus Christ (11). When old enough they should testify to being Christians by confirming the baptismal vows that were taken for them when they were babies (12).

Michael Botting
Editor

60 Blinded

AIM

To tell the story of the conversion of Saul of Tarsus.

TEXT

Acts 9:1–22.

DRAMA

Drama for all the Family 31 'Home Improvements'. Also
Scripture Union sound-strip or video *On Fire* part 5
'Blinded'. If a video can be easily shown in church,
then part of the Scripture Union video *All or Nothing*
might be shown.

HYMNS

The eighth-century Irish 'Be thou my vision' modernised
by Jubilate Hymns to 'Lord, be my vision, supreme in my
heart'; Richard Bewes' 'Which way are you choosing?'
(in *Youth Praise*).

PRAYERS

Alternative Service Book 1980, p 745, Collect appointed
for the Conversion of St Paul.

MAIN TALK

Preparation

Have the following three words, with accompanying simple visuals, which can either be on OHP acetates, or on cards that could be held up or placed on a teazlegraph board:

VISION—with picture of an eye

VOICE—with picture of lips

VERDICT—with picture of a T-junction road sign.

Presentation

Our story is one of the most important and well-authenticated events in the Bible, second only to the passion and resurrection of Jesus. Luke tells the story three times (Acts 9, 22, 26).

Ask who the first Christian martyr was. Saul saw Stephen die and was probably privately very impressed.

Refer to the journey to Damascus from Jerusalem, which is about 150 miles, and would take several days, giving plenty of time for Saul to reflect on what the Christians were preaching, comparing it with the message of the Old Testament, which he would know well.

Note that according to Acts 26:13 Saul was reaching Damascus about midday, so that the sun, shining on light baked earth, could be physically blinding in any case, but that does not rule out a supernatural light as well.

1. THE VISION

Ask what Saul saw. Probably a supernatural light. Tell the story of the Indian, Sundar Singh, who, like Saul, was initially bitterly opposed to the gospel. However, praying one early morning, he saw a great light. 'Then, as I prayed and looked into the light, I saw the form of the Lord Jesus Christ. It had such an appearance of glory and love. If it had been some Hindu incarnation I would have prostrated myself before it. But it was the Lord Jesus Christ whom I had been insulting a few days before. I felt a vision like this could not come out of my own imagination.'

2. THE VOICE

Ask what Saul heard. Sundar Singh's experience was similar: 'I heard a voice saying in Hindustani: "How long will you persecute me? I have come to save you. You were praying to know the right way; why do you not take it?"

The man who was to become the great bishop of the church, St Augustine of Hippo (AD 354–430), led a very sinful life as a young man. But he tells in his *Confessions*: 'I heard a voice, as if it had been some boy or girl from a house not far off, uttering and often repeating in a sing-song manner, "Take up and read, take up and read." This led directly to him picking up a Bible, opening it and reading where it fell open at Romans 13:13–14: 'Let us behave decently, as in the daytime, not in orgies and drunkenness . . . Rather, clothe yourselves with the Lord Jesus Christ, and do not think about how to gratify the desires of the sinful nature.'

3. THE VERDICT

Saul realised that Jesus had risen from the dead, as the Christians had been preaching, and everything else fell into place. He must now become a preacher of the same message.

Sundar Singh came to the same conclusion: 'Jesus Christ is not dead but living and it must be he himself. So I fell at his feet and got this wonderful peace which I could not get anywhere else. This is the joy I was wishing to get. When I got up, the vision had all disappeared, but . . . the peace and joy have remained with me ever since.'

(Note that there is no evidence that Sundar had ever heard the story of St Paul's conversion.)

C. S. Lewis, author of the Narnia books, says in his autobiography:

> You must picture me alone in that room at Magdalen, night after night, feeling, whenever my mind lifted even for a second from my work, the steady, unrelenting approach of Him whom I so earnestly desired not to meet. That which I greatly feared had at last come upon me. In the Trinity Term of 1929 I gave in, and admitted that God was God, and knelt and prayed: perhaps, that night, the most dejected and reluctant convert in all England. I did not then see what is now the most shining and obvious thing; the Divine humility which will accept a convert even on such terms. The Prodigal Son at least walked home on his own two feet. But who can but adore that Love which will open the high gates to a prodigal who is brought in kicking, struggling, resentful, and darting his eyes in every direction for a chance of escape? (*Surprised by Joy*, HarperCollins.)

End with some sort of brief appeal to those who have not reached the same verdict as Saul, Sundar, Augustine and C. S. Lewis.

Michael Botting
Editor

APPENDIX 1
Stories and Sketches

Note: The numbers in parentheses indicate the talks with which the stories or sketches may be associated.

TEDDY BROWN STORIES BY PAT ASHE

A. Toy Soldier Loses His Busby (4)
B. Camelot Learns to Say 'Thank You' (5)
C. The Bad Gang (16)
D. Mo's Fall (28)
E. Knave of Hearts Learns to Say 'Sorry' (30)
F. White Lies (34)
G. Miss Goodygood Makes Teddy Brown Cross (44)
H. The Boomerang (45)
J. The Tape Measure (56)

MISCELLANEOUS STORIES AND SKETCHES

K. The Conversion of Augustine of Hippo (9)
L. Joseph's Story (1) (11, 12, 13, 14, 15)
M. Joseph's Story (2) (11, 12, 13, 14, 15)
N. O Taste and See (10)
P. Guilty Conscience (19)
Q. Henrietta the Hen (25)
R. The Upside-Down Men (34)
S. Jasper, Caspar and George (7, 39, 40, 42)

A. Toy Soldier Loses His Busby

Toy Soldier was brushing his busby. He was very proud of it. It was a tall hat made of black bear fur, and when he wore it, it made him look big and bold and fierce. He brushed it lovingly and was polishing the chin strap.

Teddy Brown and Sad Dog Mona came in looking very wet. Mona had gone for a walk and it started to rain. On the way home she could not get over a stile. Luckily Teddy Brown heard her shouting and went to help her. They came in looking like drowned rats.

Toy Soldier looked Teddy Brown up and down. 'Your fur could do with a brush,' he said. 'You look really scruffy. I can't think what Robby sees in you.' Then he added spitefully, 'You've got no guts.'

Teddy Brown tried not to get upset. He felt like saying something nasty, but he remembered Jesus had not answered back. That made him feel better, so he did not say anything.

Robby knew that Toy Soldier and Teddy Brown did not get on very well, so he thought he would take them out together to his school fete, and see if that helped. When they got there he gave them each a £1 coin and said, 'Now you go off and have a happy time together. Meet me at the gate at four o'clock.'

Toy Soldier looked very smart in his busby. He marched around until he found a stall where you could get six wooden balls for 10p, and then throw them at a lot of cups and saucers and plates on a rack to see how many you could break. Toy Soldier thought that was brilliant, and he managed to break something with every ball he threw. After a few ten pennyworths he got rather hot, so he took off his busby and put it on the counter.

'I'll have another ten pennyworth,' he said to the stallholder. 'I'm enjoying this.'

Soon he had only 10p left. He thought he had better keep that in case he wanted to do something else, so he walked off.

And what do you think?

He forgot his busby!

In the meantime, Teddy Brown had found a stall where you could throw rings at a board, and try to get them on to hooks. If you got all six rings on, you got a prize.

It was really quite difficult, but Teddy Brown held the ring up, closed one eye and then the other eye, took aim and threw, and the ring landed on a hook. He did that each time, and all six rings landed on hooks.

The lady running the stall said, 'You must have had a lot of practice.'

'No,' said Teddy Brown, 'it's the first time I've ever done it.'

'Beginner's luck,' she said. 'Anyway, you've won a nice prize.' And she picked up a box with a brand new train set in it. It had an engine, four carriages and a long piece of track.

Teddy Brown's eyes grew wide with pleasure. 'Ooh,' he gasped, 'I've always wanted a train set.' And he hugged it to his chest.

He met Toy Soldier. 'Hello, Toy Soldier. Look what I've just won!'

'Um, not bad,' said Toy Soldier.

'Where's your busby?'

Toy Soldier's hand flew to his head. 'Oh, my busby,' he wailed. 'I've left it at the crockery stall.'

He rushed back. There was nothing on the counter. 'Where's my busby?' he shouted at the man.

'Dunno,' the stallholder said. 'Someone must have pinched it.'

Toy Soldier was in a panic. He rushed around looking for anyone who might have his busby. He passed the white elephant stall that had all sorts of bits and pieces on it—ornaments, old toys, old tools, some pictures—and there on the stall Toy Soldier saw his busby.

It had a price tag on it—75p.

'That's my busby!' he shouted to the man.

'Could be,' the man said. 'Could be yours if you pay me seventy five-pence.'

'It's mine—I've just lost it.'

The man shook his head. 'Seventy-five pence,' he repeated.

Toy Soldier only had 10p left. He needed another 65p. He dashed off to look for Robby, but could not find him anywhere. Then he saw Teddy Brown. He did not think Teddy Brown would be willing to lend him any money as he had been so horrid to him.

'Teddy Brown, please can you lend me 65p? I've lost my busby, and I want to buy it back.'

Teddy Brown rubbed his nose and scratched his ear. Then he said, 'Yes, I'll lend it to you.'

As they hurried back to the white elephant stall, Toy Soldier saw a boy carrying his busby.

'Look,' said Toy Soldier, 'that boy's got my busby.' He went up to the boy. 'That's my busby.'

'No it's not,' said the boy. 'It's mine—I've just bought it. I paid seventy-five pence for it.'

Teddy Brown did some quick thinking. He worked out that between them they had £1—his 90p, and Toy Soldier's 10p.

'I'll tell you what,' he said to the boy. 'We'll buy it

from you for more than you paid—we'll give you a pound.'

'No,' said the boy, 'it's mine. I want it, and I'm going to keep it.'

Toy Soldier was on the verge of tears. He could not threaten to bash the boy and take it from him as he was too big. The boy started to walk away.

At that moment Teddy Brown said, 'What about a swap?' And he held out the train set. The boy stopped. 'This old hat for a train set? Yes, OK.'

Teddy Brown handed over his train set, and Toy Soldier took the busby. He put it on his head and tried to look fierce, but there was a tear in his eye, and his moustache was drooping.

'Thanks, Teddy Brown,' he said. 'Thanks very much.' And he turned away so as not to let Teddy Brown see the tear.

That evening Toy Soldier went and found Teddy Brown.

'Why did you do it?' he asked. 'Why did you give away your train set for me?'

Teddy Brown said, 'I didn't want to at first. But then I remembered how lonely and lost I used to feel before I came to live in the Toy Cupboard. Here I learned about Jesus, and found so many friends who loved me.'

Toy Soldier felt as if he might cry again.

Teddy Brown went on, 'Then I remembered that Jesus gave his whole life for people who were horrible to him, and they killed him. And what's a train set compared to that?'

Toy Soldier's moustache began drooping. He did not dare say anything in case his voice went funny.

Teddy Brown went on, 'I know you've been horrid to me sometimes, and it has often made me cross. But when I thought about Jesus I felt he said to me, "You may not love Toy Soldier, but I do, so I will help you to love him too." Then I knew I must give my train set for your busby.'

Toy Soldier's voice cracked, 'Thanks—thanks very much, Teddy Brown.'

Toy Soldier soon got back to his old shouting ways, but from then on he never said unkind things to Teddy Brown.

B. Camelot Learns to Say 'Thank You'

One day a new animal came to live in the Toy Cupboard. He was a camel, and Robby called him Camelot. He always walked around with his nose in the air, and looked down on all the others. He expected everyone to do things for him and never said 'Thank you'. He did not see why he should.

When he had a birthday and got some presents, Robby said to him, 'Camelot, what about saying "Thank you"?' But Camelot said, 'Why should I? It's my birthday. People are supposed to give presents on birthdays.'

At Christmas he would not say 'Thank you'. He said, 'It's Father Christmas' job to bring presents at Christmas.'

And when he got lost, and a policeman brought him home, he would not say 'Thank you'. He stuck his nose in the air and said, 'Policemen are paid for doing that.'

But he began to find that although he thought everyone ought to give him things, and do things for him, a lot of the other toys stopped bothering about him. One day Elephant was giving a party, and did not invite Camelot. Camelot got very cross and rude to Elephant, and said, 'You've *got* to invite me.'

But Elephant just took a swipe at him with his trunk.

The longer Camelot stayed in the Toy Cupboard, the more upset and angry he got. He kept on saying, 'I've got a *right* to that.' Or, 'You've got no *right* to leave me out.'

He thought he was the most important toy in the Toy

Cupboard, and he just could not understand why the other toys did not like him.

Then he noticed that everyone seemed to like Teddy Brown. He did not think much of Teddy Brown, but the others always seemed to want to be with him. He never looked lonely, and the others always asked him to their parties, and gave him things. Camelot wondered what they saw in him, so he watched him.

He noticed that whenever Teddy Brown said 'Thank you', he said it as if he really meant it. He said 'Thank you' as if he were surprised that anyone would want to ask him to a party. He said 'Thank you' as if he wondered why anyone would want to give him a present. He seemed genuinely pleased whenever anyone did anything for him.

It made Camelot wonder.

One lovely sunny afternoon the toys had all gone down to have a picnic by the stream. Robby had told them to be very careful as the stones were slippery. A group of them had wandered down the stream following a beautiful butterfly that kept fluttering away just as they got near it.

Camelot had his nose in the air, and was telling them that the butterflies in the country he came from were much bigger and better. He had his nose up so high, that he did not see where he was going and—splash—he fell into the stream.

The toys stood round watching.

'Help!' shouted Camelot. But no one moved. 'Help, I'm drowning!' he bubbled.

Teddy Brown shouted to Giraffe, 'Giraffe, you can run fastest; go and get Robby, quick.'

Giraffe galloped off, and soon Robby came running up. Just a few bubbles were coming up from the bottom of the stream. Robby jumped right in, put his arm down and grabbed Camelot by his neck. He pulled him out and then squeezed the water out of him.

Camelot opened his eyes. 'Oh thank you, Robby—thank you ever so much for saving me.'

'You can also thank Teddy Brown and Giraffe for coming to get me.'

Camelot did not find that so easy.

'Nice of you to go and get Robby,' he mumbled.

Robby had got so wet that he caught a nasty cold, and was in bed for a couple of days. Camelot and Teddy Brown were sitting on his bed. Robby was reading his Bible.

'What does it say, Robby?'

Robby read them the bit he was reading: 'Thank God at all times for everything in the name of the Lord Jesus Christ.'*

A few days later, Camelot got Teddy Brown on his own.

'Why is it so important to say "Thank you"? Did you always find it so easy?'

Teddy Brown rubbed his nose, and scratched his ear while he thought hard. 'No,' he said, 'I used to think everyone should run round me, and I used to get really cross if I was left out of things. But then Robby told me God loved me.'

'Why did that help you to say "Thank you"?'

'I realised how difficult it must be for God to love me, and I saw how horrid and selfish I was. Then when I discovered that he had actually come as Jesus and died on the cross for me, I thought he must want me to be very different from what I was.'

'So what did you do?'

'I asked Jesus to change my heart, and since then I have been so grateful to Jesus that it has made me grateful to everyone else.'

'Since Robby saved me, I've really wanted to be the

* Ephesians 5:20

sort of camel that can say "Thank you", but it's ever so difficult. Do you think Jesus could change me?'

Teddy Brown knew that he could—so together they asked Jesus to put his Spirit into Camelot's heart. And Camelot began to change. He stopped walking about with his nose in the air. He found he wanted to say 'Thank you', and it really came from his heart.

C. The Bad Gang

Black-and-white Tiger was always picking on Knave of Hearts, and as he grew older he became more and more growly, snarly and bad tempered. He growled at any of the toys who had asked Jesus to direct their lives. He really resented those who had asked Jesus into their hearts, and whenever they did anything that Tiger did not like, he would snarl, 'Call yourself a Christian!' or 'You're a rotten hypocrite.'

This worried Pink Rabbit and Teddy Brown, and they used to ask Jesus to show them if Tiger was right, and how they needed to change.

Some way down the road on the edge of the wood, there lived a boy who had several of those toys that look like monsters—green, with big mouths and long fangs, dinosaurs with rows of horrible teeth, crocodiles, Daleks and weird creatures from outer space. Some of these toys got together and called themselves 'The Bad Gang'. They used to wander round the wood looking for trouble. Robby's toys kept away from them, and if ever they saw them in the wood, they used to run and hide. Even Toy Soldier and Elephant avoided them.

One day Bulldog, who had become very well-mannered and thoughtful since he had asked Jesus to come into his life, came back from a walk and said, 'The Bad Gang is in the wood—we'd all better keep away.'

Tiger growled, and then turned on Bulldog, 'Since you

269

became a Christian you've gone soft—you're afraid of that gang.'

Bulldog said, 'Well, I'm not spoiling for a fight, and I don't think fighting them would make any difference.'

Tiger gave a half snort, half growl. 'You Christians are just a lot of softies.'

Pink Rabbit nearly said, 'What about Teddy Brown? He wasn't a softie when he faced up to Cholmondley the Chinese Lion.' But she thought she had better keep quiet.

Bulldog said, 'It's not that we are soft, Tiger, but we know that if we really want someone to change, we have to love them. Saint Paul said, "If your enemy is hungry, feed him. If he is thirsty, give him a drink." '*

Tiger shouted, 'Oh, stop preaching. You know very well that doesn't work.'

Bulldog said firmly, 'But Tiger, I know it does work.'

Tiger went off growling and swishing his tail.

Tiger decided to go for a walk in the woods just to show them that he was not afraid of any Bad Gang, so he put on his fiercest look and went out.

He had just come to a rather dark part of the wood, when suddenly the Bad Gang jumped on him, yelling at the tops of their voices. They bit him, tore him and beat him—and although he fought like the tiger he was, there were too many for him. They left him lying on the ground unconscious.

When he came round he could not walk. He crawled into the shelter of a rock and thought he was going to die.

When Tiger did not return that night, the toys thought they had better tell Robby, so in the morning Teddy Brown went along and told him.

'I wonder what could have happened to him,' Robby said. 'It's not like Tiger to stay out all night. You'd better

---

* Romans 12:20

make up a search party, and if you have not found him by the time I get back from school, I'll come and join in the search.'

When Teddy Brown asked for volunteers, Pink Rabbit, Bulldog and Giraffe said they would go. Yusuf said, 'I wouldn't go if I were you. You might get caught by the Bad Gang.'

Teddy Brown said a prayer before they left, and asked Jesus to help them find Tiger, but it was not till the afternoon that they came across the Black-and-white Tiger. He was only just alive.

Teddy Brown took charge.

'Giraffe, run as fast as you can and tell Robby. He should be back from school by now. And when you come back bring the first aid kit. Bulldog, you run down to the stream, and find something to bring water in.'

Pink Rabbit was hopping about not knowing what to do. Teddy Brown said, 'Now, Pink Rabbit, you just keep calm, and put your paw on Tiger's forehead and say a prayer for him.'

It was not long before Giraffe was back with the first aid kit, and Bulldog had found an old tin can which he washed out and filled with water. Teddy Brown began washing Tiger's wounds very tenderly and gently. Bulldog ran down for some more water and held it to Tiger's lips.

When Robby arrived he carried Tiger very carefully, so that no more of his stuffing should come out. He put him into a cardboard shoe-box with some cotton-wool at the bottom to make him comfortable. They called in the nurse, and Bert the Barber had to get busy with his needle and thread. But the ones who took most trouble with Tiger were Teddy Brown, Pink Rabbit and Giraffe. They sat with him, and held his paw when he could not get to sleep, and Bulldog visited him every day.

Tiger began to feel better.

Then he remembered that he was a tiger, and tigers should growl and snarl. So he growled at Teddy Brown and said, 'You've forgotten to give me my pills.'

And he snapped at Pink Rabbit and said, 'Keep your silly paws off me.'

But they did not seem to mind, and went on helping him.

One day, when Robby came in to see him, Tiger said, 'Robby I don't think my tiger nature is very nice. I am being really nasty to some of the toys, but they just go on being friendly.'

Robby said, 'You know, Tiger, we all need to change our natures. I had to get rid of my human nature, and ask Jesus to give me a new one. Teddy Brown had to get rid of his bear nature when he asked Jesus into his heart. And Pink Rabbit exchanged her rabbit nature for the new one Jesus gave her. That is what Bulldog did, and Giraffe. They are letting the new nature take over and grow in them.'

'I know they are different. They have become kind and strong somehow, and even when I am really nasty to them, it does not make them cross or unhappy. That is what used to make me so cross with them. But I know now that they have found something I wish I could find.'

Robby said, 'They have discovered that Jesus is alive, and can start changing their natures.'

'I'd like Jesus to do that for me.'

So Robby and Black-and-white Tiger prayed together, and Tiger asked Jesus to take control of his life and give him a new nature.

And that is how Tiger began to change.

D. Mo's Fall

Near where Robby lived there were some very high rocks and crags, and Mo the Monkey used to go off climbing. He was very good at rock climbing, and when he came back he would say to the others, 'It's wonderful—so exciting. It's such fun—you ought to try it.'

He got them all saying that they would like to go rock climbing too.

Teddy Brown, Toy Soldier and Pink Rabbit got very keen, so they went to Robby and said, 'Please Robby, may we go rock climbing?'

'Oh, I don't think that's a very good idea,' Robby said. 'It's really quite dangerous. If you go you would have to do it properly, with ropes and a guide.'

'I'm sure Mo would take us,' said Pink Rabbit. 'He often goes, and says he knows the rocks like the back of his hand.'

So finally Robby agreed, and asked Mo if he would lead them and be their guide.

One early morning they set off with some sandwiches and a long rope to tie themselves together, so that if one fell, the others would be able to stop him falling right down to the bottom. Mo was so proud of himself as a climber that he thought he could never fall and that he did not need a rope. He said to himself, 'I'm sure one of those sillies will fall and then they will drag me down with them. I know what I'll do—I'll just pretend to tie a knot round myself, then if they fall, they won't drag me down.'

So Toy Soldier, Teddy Brown and Pink Rabbit tied themselves together and gave the other end of the rope to Mo the Monkey to tie round himself. He pretended to do so and then they set off with Mo leading.

Mo kept looking round to see if one of them was going to fall. But in doing that, he did not look what he was doing and suddenly *he* slipped and fell. The others held on tight expecting to feel the jerk when he got to the end of the rope—but nothing happened! Mo fell right down and the rope just dangled loose. Luckily he stuck on a ledge, but he broke his arm, and his leg was all twisted under him, and he had banged his head. Pink Rabbit looked down and said, 'Oh poor Mo!' and then she shouted, 'Mo, you must try and climb up. Oh Mo, do try!'

But all Mo did was to give a groan.

Toy Soldier said, 'I wonder if he didn't tie the rope on purpose. That rotten Mo. I bet he never tied it round himself in case one of us fell. Serves him right. Let's leave him there.' He began twisting his moustache. 'That Monkey thinks he's so clever. Now see where his pride's got him.'

Teddy Brown was looking down the cliff to where Mo was stuck. 'I know,' he said. 'Let's let the rope down and Mo can tie himself on and we'll pull him up.'

So they let down the rope and Pink Rabbit shouted, 'Mo, tie the rope round your waist and we'll pull you up.'

But Mo's arm was broken and he could not move. All he did was groan.

Teddy Brown said, 'Someone will have to go down and tie him on—then we can pull him up.'

The other two agreed but did not offer. Toy Soldier said, 'What about you, Brown? You're always looking for a good turn to do.'

Teddy Brown said, 'All right, I'll go. You two will have to let me down slowly until I reach the ledge.'

So they tied the rope around Teddy Brown's waist and then let him down till he reached the ledge. Mo was quite helpless, so Teddy Brown undid the rope that was round himself and tied it round Mo. Then he called up, 'Pull him up, but very carefully.'

So Toy Soldier and Pink Rabbit pulled Mo up till they got him where it was safe. Then they let the rope down again and hauled up Teddy Brown.

They carried Mo back and made him comfortable in the Toy Cupboard and then everyone wanted to know what had happened.

Toy Soldier was stamping around shouting, 'That silly Mo could have got us all killed. If I'd had my way we'd have left him where he was.'

Teddy Brown hardly said anything, but Pink Rabbit was hopping round saying that Teddy Brown was a hero and had risked his life to save Mo.

Robby and his dad were listening and when the excitement had died down, everyone noticed that Dad was looking very thoughtful.

'D'you know,' he said, 'what happened to Mo the Monkey is really what happened to all the people in the world. They thought they could do without God and they disobeyed him. It's called "The Fall".'

Robby said, 'I've read about that. It's at the beginning of the Bible.'

Robby's dad went on, 'That's right—everyone in the world became like Mo was—helpless and not able to save themselves.'

'Mo's arm's broken,' said Pink Rabbit. 'He couldn't tie himself on.'

But Dad continued, 'God could have done one of three things: he could have been like you, Toy Soldier and said, "It's your own fault—I'm just going to leave you to die."'

Mo looked at Toy Soldier and whispered, 'Sorry.' Toy Soldier went very red and his moustache began to droop.

'Or,' said Dad, 'he could have done what you did, Pink Rabbit and shouted good advice: "You must climb out of the mess you are in." But man was too far gone. Like you, Mo, he just could not climb out.'

They were all listening to Robby's dad as he went on. 'But what God *did* do was what you did, Teddy Brown. He came down himself as Jesus. He has reached down from heaven and given everyone a chance of being saved.'

Teddy Brown rubbed his nose and scratched his ear. He was thinking. Then he said, 'When I asked Jesus to take over my life, it was like being tied to a lifeline and he pulled me out of the mess I was getting into.'

Toy Soldier turned his eyes up as if to say, 'There goes Brown again bringing religion into everything,' but he did not say anything, because all the others had been listening very carefully to what Robby's dad had been saying.

E. Knave of Hearts Learns to Say 'Sorry'

A long time ago, before Jack the Knave of Hearts became a Christian, he had put a stocking over his face, beaten up Yusuf the rich doll from Persia, stolen his silver buttons and taken all the money from his pockets.

No one knew who had done it, but after Knave of Hearts became a Christian he began to get twinges of conscience. A little voice in his mind kept saying, 'You really ought to do something about Yusuf.' And he noticed that he felt particularly guilty when he was saying his prayers.

One day he spoke to Teddy Brown about it. He said, 'You remember Yusuf had his silver buttons stolen?'

'Yes,' said Teddy Brown.

'Well, I'm afraid I stole them.'

Teddy Brown looked suitably shocked, though he had guessed it a long time ago.

'Do you think I ought to do anything about it?'

Teddy Brown rubbed his nose and scratched his ear—he was thinking.

Then Knave of Hearts went on, 'I suppose I could just leave his buttons on his bed when no one was looking.'

Teddy Brown did not think that was good enough. He thought Knave of Hearts should also own up and say he was sorry.

Knave did not like that idea much, but he said, 'Well, I suppose if I give him back his buttons and any money I took, he should be all right about it.'

Teddy Brown was not sure about that, but they went along together and found Yusuf.

Knave of Hearts said, 'I say, Yusuf old man, I think I ought to tell you that I took your buttons, and now that I'm a Christian I would like to give them back. I'm sorry about it, but I hope you won't hold it against me. And would you mind not letting any of the other toys know, as I would not like to spoil my reputation.'

Teddy Brown thought to himself, 'Oh dear, I'm afraid he's not doing it right at all.'

Yusuf turned on Knave in an absolute fury, 'You rotten thief!' he shouted. 'You're a criminal. You ought to be locked up or thrown out of the Toy Cupboard. I'm going to tell Robby and all the others, and I hope none of them ever speak to you again.'

Knave of Hearts was shocked. He said, 'Well, I've said I'm sorry. But it really was partly your fault, you know.'

'My fault!' Yusuf yelled. 'What d'you mean—my fault?'

'Well, you were always showing off your silver buttons and jingling the money in your pocket. That was putting temptation in people's way. No wonder you got robbed.'

Yusuf was speechless with rage. Then he spluttered, 'You're not going to get away with this. I'll get you thrown into the dustbin.'

This made Knave of Hearts cross. He said, 'No need to turn nasty. I've said I'm sorry, and if you were a decent chap you'd have accepted my apology and shaken hands.'

At this, Yusuf clenched his fists, and was just going to punch the Knave when Toy Soldier came up. He pushed them apart.

'Just stop that, you two. No fighting in the Toy Cupboard without my permission.'

Teddy Brown groaned. 'Oh dear,' he thought. 'He couldn't have done it worse.'

When they were alone, Knave of Hearts said to Teddy Brown, 'What did I do wrong? I said I was sorry. What more did he want?'

Teddy Brown said, 'First of all, when you say you are sorry, you have got to be *really* sorry. Then you apologise humbly, and if the other person turns nasty, you are ready to take it.'

Knave thought about that, and then he remembered the question that Robby was always telling him to ask. He said, 'I wonder how Jesus would have said it?' He thought a bit more, and then he said to Teddy Brown, 'I don't think Jesus would have said it quite like I did.'

Teddy Brown gave a sigh, and a little thank you to Jesus. Then he said, 'Robby showed me something in his Bible the other day. It said that when Jesus suffered for something he had not done, he did not threaten, but took it patiently.'

'I'm afraid Yusuf made me cross,' said the Knave.

'And another thing,' said Teddy Brown. 'You said "But". You must *never* say "But" after apologising. It just starts up the row again.'

Knave of Hearts was very sorry he had made such a mess of his apology, and he went off to be alone with Jesus. After he had had a little talk with Jesus, he saw what he had done wrong.

Next time he met Yusuf he said, 'I'm terribly sorry— please forgive me. I'll pay back everything I took from you. I know that won't undo the fact that I stole it, and that I hurt you. I just want you to know that I really am very very sorry.'

Yusuf scowled at him, but he did not start shouting again, because he realised that Knave was really sorry.

After Knave had paid everything back, Yusuf did not feel quite so angry with him, though he found it impossible to forgive him, because Yusuf had never asked Jesus into his heart.

F.   White Lies

Teddy Brown, Pink Rabbit and Dutch Doll had gone to church with Robby, and the reading was from St Paul's letter to the Romans. They could not understand much of it, but they remembered the last verse: 'The wages of sin is death, but the gift of God is eternal life through Jesus.'

When they got home Pink Rabbit asked Robby, 'What is sin?'

Robby thought about that for a minute, then he said, 'Sin is not being like Jesus.'

'That's very difficult,' said Dutch Doll, 'because we've never met him.'

Robby said, 'No, but people who knew him have written lots about him, so we can read what Jesus did and said.'

'But I can't read,' said Pink Rabbit.

'Most people couldn't read at one time. That is one of the reasons why they had vicars who could read, and they explained things in sermons,' said Robby.

Teddy Brown said, 'Even if you can't read, when you ask Jesus into your heart you know whether things are right or wrong. We usually know when we are not being like him.'

Pink Rabbit said, 'I don't do wrong things like Knave of Hearts used to do. I don't steal things, but I know I'm not like Jesus. Does that mean I'm a sinner, Robby?'

'Yes,' said Robby. 'The Bible says we are all sinners because not one of us is like Jesus. He never sinned.'

Teddy Brown said, 'I once heard someone say, "Sin is sin, whether it is big or little." Do you think that is true, Robby?'

Dutch Doll interrupted, 'Oh I don't think it is. Surely there is a difference between a white lie and a whopper. Surely it is all right to tell a fib now and then.'

Pink Rabbit looked puzzled. 'What's a fib?' she asked.

'Oh, just little things like saying you didn't hear her call when Mummy wanted you to help with the washing up; or saying that your pearls are real when they are fake.'

Pink Rabbit said, 'I can't imagine Jesus telling fibs, can you, Robby?'

'No, I can't,' said Robby. 'And that's why we ought not to.'

The next week there was great excitement because they were all going on holiday to the Scilly Isles, and they were going to fly. It was the first time some of them had been in an aeroplane, and they were just a little bit frightened, though none of them would admit it.

Pink Rabbit shut her eyes tight while the plane took off, but when it had got well up she began to look out of the window. She said, 'Look at all those tiny little houses. I wonder what they are for. Do you think ants live in them, Teddy Brown?'

'Don't be silly, Pink Rabbit, they are ordinary houses: bungalows, or houses with two storeys or four storeys. Some might even be tower blocks with twenty storeys.'

Pink Rabbit looked down, 'They all look the same to me from up here. I can't see whether they are big or little.'

That reminded Robby of what they had been talking about on Sunday. He turned to his dad. 'Dad, we were talking about sin on Sunday, and Dutch Doll thinks little sins don't matter—that it's all right to tell fibs.'

Dad said, 'When you look out of the window, you just see buildings. From this height you can't tell whether it is a bungalow or a ten-storey block. And when God looks down from heaven, he sees sin as sin, and it is only the result— what happens after—that makes them big or little.'

Toy Soldier said, 'What do you mean by the result making them big or little? I don't get it.'

'Well,' said Dad, 'if someone upsets you, and you get angry and hit him, but not very hard, the result is not very serious. But if you poke his eye out, the result for the person who has lost an eye is *very* serious. But both of them started with getting upset and angry—which Jesus would not have done.'

'I see what you mean,' Robby said. 'The sin was getting angry. It was the result that made it big or little. Do you understand, Teddy Brown?'

'I think so,' said Teddy Brown rather doubtfully.

Robby went on, 'One day I went to help on the farm, and the farmer asked me to dig out dandelions. I dug out a pile of really big ones, but when I showed them to him he said, "That's fine, but you have to dig out the little ones as well as the big ones, because, you see, the little ones grow big!"'

Dad said, 'That is why it's important not to tell fibs, because fibs are lies, and often one leads to another. You have to tell a bigger one to get out of the first one, and by the end of the day it has turned into a whopper. There is a saying: "Oh what a tangled web we weave when once we practise to deceive."'

That night when they all went to bed they had a talk after prayers, and some of them decided that, as they wanted to grow to be like Jesus, they would ask him to make them absolutely honest like he was. And when they were not sure what to do, they would ask themselves the question, 'What would Jesus do?' And when they did wrong, they would say 'sorry' to Jesus.

And do you know what happens then? Jesus gives you a hug, and reminds you not to do it again.

G. Miss Goodygood Makes Teddy Brown Cross

Teddy Brown had become crotchety lately. Sometimes he got quite bad tempered. He snapped at Pink Rabbit, and got sulky and moody—more like he had been before he had asked Jesus into his heart.

Pink Rabbit was quite worried and tried to have a little talk with him, but Teddy Brown said, 'Oh, you don't understand.' And then he went all silent.

Pink Rabbit decided the best thing to do was to pray for him. Then she noticed that Teddy Brown was always worse after Miss Goodygood had been about. If he saw her, he went the other way and when she came into the Toy Cupboard he went out.

Pink Rabbit wondered why, because Miss Goodygood never did anything wrong. She used to hunt through the Bible for any rules or laws she could find and make a point of keeping them. She never did anything on Saturdays because in the Bible it says, 'Keep holy the Sabbath day. In it thou shalt do no manner of work.'

But she wanted the others to do nothing on Sundays, because they counted that as their Sabbath. When the younger toys started running around, she used to say,

> 'This is Sunday, Sabbath day,
> That is why you must not play,
> Nor run about and make a noise,
> Like the naughty girls and boys.'

And she made up a lot of rules of her own: Never wear lipstick or powder. Never go to the cinema. Never eat sweets in Lent. Never listen to pop music. Never play cards.

One day Pink Rabbit screwed up courage and asked Teddy Brown, 'Why does Miss Goodygood make you so cross?'

Teddy Brown exploded, 'Oh, she's so self-righteous. She's always judging others and making herself out to be so holy with all her rules and laws—and expecting everyone else to keep them. She looks down her nose at the rest of us. I can't bear her.'

Pink Rabbit was amazed at this outburst. She had never seen Teddy Brown so upset. She did not dare say, 'Have a little talk with Jesus,' but she said, 'Why don't you have a talk with Robby?'

'I might,' said Teddy Brown and went off under the piano.

A few days later Teddy Brown went and saw Robby, and told him how upset he was with Miss Goodygood. Robby listened to it all, and then he said, 'Of course you are judging her as much as she is judging you. You know she is wrong, but you are not a hundred per cent right yourself. You have let her come between you and Jesus.'

Teddy Brown went off feeling miserable, but he knew he ought to have a talk with Jesus. So he went away on his own and thought about Jesus. And as he thought about Jesus he began to feel quiet and peaceful inside. It was as if something hard had begun to melt. He remembered the chorus they sang in church: 'Turn your eyes upon Jesus, look full in his wonderful face, and the things of earth will grow strangely dim, in the light of his glory and grace.'

He saw that he had let Miss Goodygood come between him and Jesus, and he began to feel very sorry.

Just then Robby called them to go to church.

After the service, Teddy Brown knelt down to talk to Jesus, and as he was right down below the pew, he could not be seen. He heard Miss Goodygood talking to Dutch Doll.

'You see, I keep all the rules,' she was saying. 'I never tell a lie. I go to church every Sunday. I say my prayers morning and evening. I give away a tenth of my pocket money. I know God is pleased with me. I'm not like Knave of Hearts who used to steal, or Pink Rabbit who forgets to say grace, or like Teddy Brown who does not think you have to keep any of the rules.'

Dutch Doll was not as empty-headed as some thought. She said, 'St Augustine said "Love God, and do what you like."'

Miss Goodygood was amazed—not only because Dutch Doll knew about St Augustine but also that he should have said that.

'What on earth did he mean?'

'Well, you see,' said Dutch Doll, 'if you love God you won't do anything that hurts him, so you will really like to do what he wants.'

Miss Goodygood said, 'That all sounds so simple—but I don't find being a Christian is simple. I find it hard to remember to keep all the rules.'

Dutch Doll thought for a moment, then she said, 'Serving Jesus is supposed to set you free, not tie you up with a lot of rules.'

Miss Goodygood looked down her nose at Dutch Doll. 'You seem to be taking Teddy Brown's side.'

'I'm not taking his side. But perhaps Teddy Brown has discovered something that we have missed.'

Miss Goodygood then lifted her nose in the air, and walked off.

Teddy Brown stayed on praying. Then he whispered, 'O

God, I'm sorry. I have fallen away from Jesus.' Then he sang very softly —

'Into my heart, into my heart
Come into my heart, Lord Jesus.
Come in today,
Come in to stay,
Come into my heart, Lord Jesus.'

Then he prayed, 'Lord Jesus, thank you for forgiving me. I have been so miserable separated from you, and I have made others miserable too. Thank you for coming back into my heart.'

He felt so much happier that he went to Miss Goodygood and said, 'I'm sorry I have been avoiding you. I was wrong to feel as I did, and I have asked Jesus to forgive me. Will you forgive me too?'

Miss Goodygood stammered, 'Oh, er, yes—yes of course.'

But she was not quite sure what Teddy Brown was talking about. She went away wondering whether Dutch Doll was right—perhaps Teddy Brown had discovered something about Jesus that she had missed.

H.   The Boomerang

One day Robby threw something into the Toy Cupboard, and shut the door. It was a funny wooden thing shaped rather like a flat banana.

They all had a look at it, but no one knew what it was. While they were wondering, Toy Soldier who always thought he knew everything, marched up. He said, 'It isn't anything special—it just happens to be that shape.'

Pink Rabbit said, 'I don't like the look of it. It makes me feel creepy.'

Just then Kangaroo came up, and she knew immediately what it was, because she had been made in Australia.

'I know what that is,' she said. 'It's a boomerang.'

None of them had ever heard of a boomerang, so she might just as well have said, 'It's a pangwangle.'

'What's a boomerang?' asked the Knave of Hearts.

'This is a boomerang,' said Kangaroo, delighted.

Teddy Brown tried. 'What Knave means is, what is a boomerang for?'

So Kangaroo explained. 'If you throw it at an animal or a person and it does not hit them, it comes back to you, and then you can throw it again.'

'That's a lot of rot,' said Toy Soldier. 'I don't believe it.' He picked up the boomerang and threw it. It whizzed through the air in a big circle and came sailing back. Toy Soldier was not expecting it, and it gave him a real whack on the head and knocked him down. He stumped off to his room, furious.

Pink Rabbit found him on his bed moaning. 'The beastly thing came back and hit me,' he said.

'But Kangaroo told you it would come back.'

Toy Soldier scowled, but Pink Rabbit went on, 'She had a lovely time throwing the boomerang and catching it.'

Robby and Teddy Brown came in to see how Toy Soldier was.

'Hullo, Toy Soldier,' said Robby. 'I hear you have had an encounter with a boomerang. It's funny how they come back at you, but I suppose it is not only boomerangs that come back.'

Toy Soldier just grunted, and Robby and Teddy Brown went back to where the other toys were.

Pink Rabbit said, 'I remember once, Robby, you had a boomerang come back. You said, "Mum, can I have some tomato ketchup?" and you thought she was going to go and get it for you. But she said, "Yes dear, run and get it."'

That made Robby laugh. 'You cheeky thing,' he said. 'But you are quite right, it was a boomerang.'

Knave of Hearts had not thought of that as being a boomerang.

Pink Rabbit went on, 'D'you remember, Knave of Hearts, when you hit your ball into Mrs Smith's garden and broke her window? You wanted Robby to go and get it, but he said, "You go, Knave of Hearts, and say 'sorry' to Mrs Smith."'

Knave of Hearts gave a shudder. He did not want to remember that encounter with Mrs Smith. He said, 'Yes, I suppose that was a boomerang. I thought I'd thrown it at Robby, but it came right back at me.'

They began to think of other things that were like boomerangs. Teddy Brown said, 'Come to think of it, the Lord's Prayer is a series of boomerangs. We say it as if we are telling God what to do, and he throws it right back at us.'

Pink Rabbit asked, 'How does "Our Father" become a boomerang?'

Teddy Brown rubbed his nose and scratched his ear. He was thinking, but he could not quite work it out. He said, 'Do you know what I mean, Robby?'

Robby said, 'Yes, I think I do, but perhaps we'd better go and ask Dad.'

They found Dad in his study.

'Dad,' Robby said, 'Teddy Brown has had a rather funny idea. He says the Lord's Prayer is like a lot of boomerangs.'

Dad put his pen down. 'D'you know, I think he's got something there. When we say "Hallowed be thy name," it sounds as if we are saying to God, "Make everyone respect you." But God says "What are *you* doing to make my name holy? Do you honour and obey me?" So it is a sort of boomerang.'

Knave of Hearts said, 'I always thought "Thy kingdom come, thy will be done" was telling God to hurry up and take over the world. How do you make that into a boomerang?'

'Oh, I can see that one,' said Teddy Brown slowly. 'God says, "What are *you* doing about bringing people into my kingdom? Are *you* doing my will?"'

Robby got quite excited. "Give us this day our daily bread" means that we must see to it that everyone has enough food to eat.'

Dad said, 'And "Forgive us our trespasses as we forgive them that trespass against us" means that we've got to forgive others, or we will not be able to receive God's forgiveness.'

Teddy Brown was thinking about the next sentence—
'Lead us not into temptation.' He was rubbing his nose

and scratching his ear. They all knew that if they gave him time he would probably say something quite sensible. So they waited. Then he said, 'If we always let God lead us, then we would not fall into temptation, and he would deliver us from evil.'

Toy Soldier had come up to see what was going on. He still felt cross. 'Are you all talking religion again?' he grumbled. They wanted to tell him about prayer boomerangs, but he would not listen.

J.   The Tape Measure

Dutch Doll wanted to make herself a dress, and she found a very nice pattern. All the measurements were in feet and inches, but she could not find her tape measure. She called Teddy Brown.

'Teddy Brown, can you lend me a tape measure in inches? I've lost mine.'

'No, I'm sorry. But I could go and ask Robby.'

On the way he met Pink Rabbit. 'I'm going to borrow a tape measure in feet for Dutch Doll. I hope Robby has one.'

They found Robby talking to his dad, and while they waited Pink Rabbit said, 'I wonder why they are called feet.'

Robby's dad overheard and said, 'That's a very interesting question, Pink Rabbit. When they were deciding what measures to use in England they look the length of the king's foot, and divided it up into twelve parts—so we got feet and inches.'

Teddy Brown asked, 'What happened when they got a new king?'

'That's when the trouble started, because the new king's foot was not as long as his father's. They tried changing the length of the foot to fit the new king, but everyone got in such a muddle, that they decided on one foot and made it standard.'

'They must have had some real problems when they had several sized feet!' said Teddy Brown.

Then Dad went on. 'That's the trouble with the world. There are no fixed standards about the way people think they ought to live. The different religions tell people different things. So God came into the world himself to give everyone a fixed standard to live by.'

Robby said, 'I've always wondered about that. How do we know our Christian standard is the right one? How do we know that Buddha or Mohammed were not right?'

'They were men who gave some very good advice about life. But Christians do not just say that Jesus was the best of them all. We believe that he was different—that he was God himself who came into the world to demonstrate his standard—a measure for the whole of life, and for the whole world.'

'So that's why we measure everything by Jesus,' said Robby.

'Yes, that's why Christians always ask themselves "What would Jesus do?"'

It was all getting too difficult for Pink Rabbit, whose head was beginning to spin, so she took Teddy Brown's paw, and they left Robby and his dad talking. They went off to find someone else who might have a tape measure for Dutch Doll.

Teddy Brown said, 'I think I saw Yusuf with a measure—let's go and ask him.'

Now Yusuf came from Persia. He said, 'Oh yes, I can lend her a measure. It's a very nice one; it is based on the width of the Shah's right hand. She'll find it works beautifully.' But when they took it to Dutch Doll she said, 'That's no good—it hasn't got any feet and inches on it.'

So Teddy Brown went to Cholmondely the Chinese Lion.

'Oh, yes, I've got one. It is a combination of several measures—mostly from China. Very ancient civilisation, the Chinese—some of their measures are very good. Some bits are from Arabia. Very clever, the Arabs, you know. Well it's a bit from here there and everywhere, but it's a measure I always use.'

When Dutch Doll saw his measure, she did not think it would help her make a dress that would fit her.

So Teddy Brown tried Mo the Monkey.

'Why yes, of course I'll lend her my measure. I have a super one. It's so simple—every foot is as long as a piece of string. You can do anything you like with it.'

In desperation Teddy Brown went back to Robby. 'I have been trying to borrow a tape measure for Dutch Doll, but none of them is any good.'

Robby said, 'I've got one she can use—it's in feet and inches.'

So Dutch Doll was able to make her dress.

You can measure anything by asking a simple question: 'What would Jesus do if he were in my position?'

Or you could ask, 'What would Jesus say?'

Then you must be quiet so that he can guide your thinking.

K. The Conversion of St Augustine of Hippo

INTERVIEWER Augustine, thank you for granting us this unique interview. I understand you are not the only famous Augustine in the history of the church.

AUGUSTINE That's correct. I have a famous namesake who lived about 250 years after me and became the first Archbishop of Canterbury about 600 AD.

I. But you also became a bishop?

A. Yes, I eventually became Bishop of Hippo in North Africa.

I. Where were you born?

A. In North Africa—the country you call Algeria today.

I. Were you brought up in a Christian home?

A. My mother, Monica, was a very devout Christian and from my earliest days taught me about Jesus and what it meant to follow him. I was due to be baptised, but I had many questions and doubts and so my baptism was delayed. However, I had a very good education. I loved studying the great writers and teachers of my day. For a time I was a lecturer.

I. But you obviously became a Christian eventually. How did that happen?

A. I was seriously searching for the truth, but at the same time there were lots of temptations, as there always are. I was led into evil ways and felt I was enslaved by my sins.

One day I was weeping and crying to God, and was very sorry about the state of my life, when I heard the voice of a child in a nearby house singing. It kept on repeating a chorus; *'Take it and read, take it and read.'*

To begin with I took no notice, but then I wondered if God was speaking to me through the child. I stopped crying and thought that God was commanding me to open my book of Scripture and read the first passage on which my eyes fell.

I. So what did you do?

A. I hurried back to where I had been reading a book containing the letters of St Paul. I seized it and opened it and in silence read the first passage I saw:

Let us behave decently, as in the daytime, not in orgies and drunkenness, not in sexual immorality and debauchery, not in dissension and jealousy. Rather, clothe yourselves with the Lord Jesus Christ, and do not think about how to gratify the desires of the sinful nature.

I had no need to read more. In an instant it was as though the light of faith had flooded my life and all the darkness and doubt was dispelled.

I. Then what did you do?

A. I shared what had happened with a friend, and, of course, very specially with my mother, who was overjoyed to see her many prayers for me answered.

I. Thank you so much for sharing your remarkable story with us.

L. Joseph's Story (1)

Excuse me butting in like this, but I wanted you to know that what you are thinking about today really happened. It is not just a nice story—it really happened. I was there. And it is not just important that it happened, it is *why* it happened that is important as well. Let me explain.

I expect you have guessed who I am, with my saw, my mallet and my chisel. Yes, I'm Joseph, just an ordinary carpenter from Nazareth. It's hard to explain how I got caught up in all this, but the fact is that I did; and amazingly you can be caught up in it as well—if you want to.

Let me start at the beginning. I was in love with this girl. Mary was her name. She was a lovely girl, quite a bit younger than me, but we got on very well together. When I was repairing broken things in my carpenter's shop, I couldn't get her out of my mind. I felt I was the luckiest man in the world to love and be loved by such a good person.

I asked her dad if I could marry her, and surprisingly he said 'Yes', so we became engaged. In our country that is a binding agreement, and carries important responsibilities with it. We began to make plans for our wedding.

Everything seemed fine, and then it happened—one of the worst moments of my life. I can remember it as though it was yesterday. We were walking in the hills above Nazareth, and Mary had been rather quiet. Suddenly she stopped and said to me, 'Joe, I've got something to tell you, and it's very hard to explain, so please listen carefully. I'm expecting a baby, but I haven't . . .'

'Expecting a baby!' I said. 'That's great news, you slut. You've deceived me. I thought you loved me,' I shouted, as I ran off in total despair. I had to run off, otherwise I might have hit her. I was so angry, and so hurt.

I didn't know what to do. I walked for miles that day. I thought. I swore. I cried. I cursed. How could she do this to me? Who was the other man? Had she done it willingly, or had she been forced?

I would have to divorce her. We couldn't just break off our engagement, you see. It was a public, binding agreement. I would have to help her parents to take her away to another town. We didn't want any scandal in our small community. That's what I decided to do. I wonder what you would have done if you had been me.

That night I hardly slept at all. Thoughts were going through my mind all the time. I couldn't imagine Mary doing such a thing to me. Perhaps it was all a terrible mistake. What had she tried to explain to me? Eventually I must have fallen asleep, because I had this strange dream.

Someone was with me; a kind of bright light that was a person—and he began to speak to me.

'Joseph, son of David,' he said. I liked that start. My father isn't called David, but Jacob. However, I am a direct descendant of our greatest king, King David. Not many people realise that, or they might treat me with a bit more respect.

'Don't be afraid,' he went on, 'to take Mary to be your wife, for the child she is having is by the Holy Spirit. She will have a son. You must give him the name Jesus, because he will save his people from their sins.' Then he disappeared.

I didn't know what to think as I woke up. Was it a message from God? Or was I just dreaming what I wanted to hear? No, it had to be real. I couldn't really grasp what he meant. All I knew was that he said it was all right to go ahead and marry Mary. I was so happy. I had to dash over to see her.

Her parents were surprised to see me at 6 o'clock in the morning. They must have thought we had had a terrible row when Mary came home red-eyed the previous day.

Mary and I had another long walk and a very long talk. I said how sorry I was and told her about my dream and she told me about the angel coming to her, and how she had felt too confused to tell me about it until she knew that she really was having a child. We decided that we would stick with one another, and help each other through all the misunderstandings and sniggerings that there would be in Nazareth.

Somehow it was only then that I began to realise what was happening to us. My Mary was going to be the mother of the promised Messiah, for whom our nation had waited for so long. I couldn't believe it. We were going to have this special person growing up in our home. Our lives could never be the same again, because somehow in this baby God would be showing us himself, every day of every week. It was very exciting but very frightening at the same time.

Then I began to think about the name I had been told to give the baby—Jesus. Quite a lot of people are called Jesus. It's another form of the name Joshua, which means saviour or rescuer. This child was coming to rescue people, but not from an enemy like the Romans who marched around our land, but to save people from their sins. I thought a lot about this. What could it mean?

Gradually it dawned on me that all the wrong things that you and I do separate us from God. They spoil the friendship with God that he wants us to have. They even make us his enemies, rather than his friends. Somehow the baby that Mary was going to have was going to make it possible for me to receive forgiveness and to be friends again with God. I didn't understand then how this would happen, but I was so grateful that God was reaching out to me in his love.

Now I must be going. Just one final thought before I leave you. I had to accept Jesus as my son, even though he wasn't in fact. That was a great privilege and a great responsibility. But at times it wasn't at all easy; it was quite costly.

If Jesus' coming is going to make a difference in your life, as it has made in mine; if you are going to experience him rescuing you from the wrong things you have said and done; then I expect that in some way you will need to welcome him into your life, as I had to welcome him into mine. Today could be the day that you do this. As I had a choice about it, so do each one of you.

Enjoy the rest of your time here, and listen very carefully to everything that is said. What you hear today could change your life for ever, and I mean for ever. Not just your life now on earth, but also your life after you die.

Goodbye, and God bless. Have a good Christmas.

Peter Markby
Lewes

M. Joseph's Story (2)

I wonder if you recognise me. Yes, I am Joseph.

Do you remember how shocked I was by the news that Mary, my fianceé, was going to have a baby? But then God showed me in a vision that it was all part of his plan. Today I have been asked to tell you what happened after that.

When Mary and I had begun to get used to the idea of what was going to happen to us, we became very excited and did all the things that expectant parents do. I made a crib. Mary and her friends started knitting and making things for the new baby. We made arrangements for the village midwife to be with Mary when the time came for her to give birth. Everything was ready. Mary was becoming bigger and bigger.

Then one day our careful plans were shattered. A Roman soldier marched into our village of Nazareth and called everyone together and read out the following announcement:

> His divine excellency Caesar Augustus, ruler of the mighty Roman Empire, greets his people in every part of the world. He hopes that you appreciate the benefits of living under the peace of Rome. It seems good to him to make a register of all the people of the Empire for tax and other purposes. He requires everyone to return to their home town for the purpose of this census. Everyone must therefore be in their home town in ten days' time. This is the end of Caesar's orders. Long live Caesar Augustus.

With that he marched off and left us.

I was in despair at this news. You see I am a member of the family of David, the great King of Israel, and Bethlehem, the city of David, is our home town, but it is seventy miles from Nazareth where we live. It was a long and difficult journey for us to make, especially with Mary in her condition. I was afraid that she might lose the baby because of the arduous journey.

I felt helpless and angry that a man in Rome could give orders, which disrupted everyone's life, just because he wanted to know how many people he ruled and how he could get even more money through taxes. We hated the Romans who ruled our land. Has your country ever been occupied by another country? Have you ever had soldiers in your town ordering you around just to show you that they are in charge? It is so degrading. It is humiliating. You feel so powerless. I sometimes prayed to God to deliver us, but nothing changed. He seemed to have forgotten us.

Do you ever feel like I did? I expect you do, even if you have not got an occupying power over you. I am sure that sometimes you feel as though you have no control over your life or over your future; that someone else makes the decisions that affect you, and you feel hopeless, and that if there is a God, he does not care for you. Well, if you know any of these feelings, you will be able to understand how I felt that day when the Roman soldier made his announcement.

We had to make new arrangements as quickly as we could, and a few days later we set off for Bethlehem. I managed to borrow a donkey, so Mary could ride most of the way and avoid getting totally exhausted. We said 'Goodbye' to our friends and off we went.

It was a long journey. When we reached Bethlehem at last the place was packed with people who had come for census. It was obvious that Mary's time was very near. I searched frantically for somewhere for her to have the baby, but only managed to find a stable belonging to one of the many inns. It was not the most comfortable place to give birth, but at least it was clean and dry. Soon the labour pains began and after some hours Mary gave birth to a baby boy. We had been told that he was to be called Jesus, which means Saviour or Rescuer. We put the tiny baby in a manger, which we filled with some hay, and Mary tried to rest. As you can imagine, we were delighted that the baby had been born safely, and that all was well in spite of the journey that we had had.

A few hours later, some shepherds arrived at the stable to share our joy. They told us that angels had appeared to them while they were looking after sheep on the hills above Bethlehem. The angels told them that the Lord's promised Saviour had been born in Bethlehem. And so the baby arrived, who was going to be so special not just for us, but for people throughout the world.

Later I thought about all that had happened to us. I realised that in the birth of Jesus, God had kept his promise made to our people so long ago. If he had proved faithful in keeping that promise, perhaps we ought to trust him for the future. Maybe he had not forgotten us after all, but was waiting for the right time to keep his promise.

Then I remembered that our Scriptures say that God's rescuer would be born in Bethlehem. So though the journey from Nazareth had seemed a waste of time and just done because of the fancy of a Roman Emperor, in fact God must have been in control and used Caesar Augustus to make sure that Jesus was born in Bethlehem, and thus validate him as the promised Messiah. And it could be true for you that God is working out his purposes for you, when things happen which at first you cannot understand. That is worth trying to remember.

When I took that newborn baby in my arms, I saw a sign of hope in that baby. For in the birth of every baby there is hope. Hope that it will achieve great things; hope that it will bring joy into many people's lives; and hope that God will bless it. And I was to learn that in this child, there was hope not just for my people the Jews, but for people of every nation, for he had come to bring to all the love of God and to help us to know him better.

So the birth of Jesus brought me real hope for the future, and I pray that you will find hope today. May you find that hope which comes from welcoming the Lord Jesus Christ into your life and into your home and being ready to trust his promises for the future.

May God be with each one of you as you celebrate the birth of Jesus this Christmas. Goodbye and God bless you.

Peter Markby
Lewes

N. O Taste and See

Characters: THE PREACHER
MARKET TRADER
LADY 1
LADY 2
LADY 3
LADY 4
MAN 1
MAN 2
MAN 3

The Scene: Two stalls on a market. The main focus is on the vegetable stall where an enthusiastic trader is trying to persuade shoppers to 'buy' his goods.

TRADER Yes, madam? Square tomatoes? Ideal for making sandwiches. Four slices just fit a slice of bread. Delicious flavour. Just the thing we've been waiting for.

LADY 1 How much? You haven't put a price on them.

TRADER That's because they're free. So, lady, how many do you want?

LADY 1 Free? Impossible! If they're as good as you say, they must cost a lot.

TRADER No, lady. They're absolutely free. How many would you like?

LADY 1 None, thank you. There's got to be a catch

somewhere. If they're any good, they've got to be paid for.

[*She steps back to allow LADY 2 to approach the TRADER.*]

TRADER   Yes, madam? Would you like some square tomatoes? Just the most wonderful invention ever. Better even than sliced bread. You put them on the table and they won't roll off. How many? A pound? Two pounds?

LADY 2   How do they become square?

TRADER   Don't ask me, lady. I only sell them. I suppose the gardener developed them that way. Perhaps he grew them in square pots.

LADY 2   Or perhaps he used chemicals in the fertiliser. I don't like things grown with chemical fertilisers. It isn't natural.

TRADER   Anyhow, madam. How many would you like? They're free.

LADY 2   Free? Then they can't be any good. No, I don't want any of them, thank you. Free indeed! Nothing that was any good ever came for nothing.

[*She moves to the side and MAN 1 comes to the stall.*]

TRADER   Come along, ladies and gentlemen. Come and see the bargains I've got here. Square tomatoes, stoneless plums, and onions that don't make you cry. If you think that's too good to be true, come and try them.

MAN 1   I suppose you've also got gooseberries without whiskers?

TRADER   Now there's a coincidence. I've had some arrive this morning. Right, ladies and gentlemen. Come here and buy gooseberries

	without whiskers, onions that don't make you cry, plums without stones, and square tomatoes.
MAN 1	It's a trick, I'll bet. Some sort of a con.
TRADER	I heard that, George. You know me. You've known me since we were kids together at school, and you know I wouldn't con you.
PREACHER	He came unto his own and his own received him not. But as many as received him, to them gave he power to become the sons of God, even to them that believe on his name: which were born, not of blood, nor of the will of the flesh, nor of the will of man, but of God.
LADY 3	Anyhow, I'll bet he charges the earth for them. How much are the plums without stones?
TRADER	They're free, lady. Absolutely free.
LADY 3	Rubbish! Nothing's free in this life. [*turning to MAN 1*] I'll bet it's one of these things like *Reader's Digest* draws—you know; you think you're bound to win a fortune and everyone else gets told the same, and you all end up with no money and a room full of books on the digestive system of the Colorado beetle. I don't trust these free gifts.
MAN 2	That's right. Get a pound of these so-called free onions that don't make you cry, and you probably have a pound delivered every Friday morning whether you want them or not. [*He takes his wife's arm.*] Come on, let's see what bargain we can get over here.
PREACHER	Ho, everyone that thirsteth, come ye to the waters, and he that hath no money, come ye,

buy and eat; yea, come, buy wine and milk without money and without price.

TRADER   Come on, ladies and gentlemen. Doesn't anyone want some of these delicious square tomatoes?

LADY 4   [*Scornfully.*] Delicious square tomatoes! I'll bet they've got no flavour. That's the trouble when they muck about with things. Fancy roses lose their scent, and I'll bet it's the same with your fancy square tomatoes—no flavour.

TRADER   Try one, madam. Taste it and I'm sure you'll find it the most delicious tomato you've ever tasted. Think of the nicest thing you've ever eaten—well, it's better than that.

Come on. Won't you give it a try even? Just one mouthful and you won't be able to resist more.

MAN 3   That's it. It's addictive. I'm having nothing to do with it.

[*He moves off to next stall.*]

PREACHER Oh taste and see that the Lord is good. Blessed is the man that trusteth in him.

J. Lloyd
Leicester

P. Guilty Conscience

Characters: SATAN
                 HUMAN
                 GOD

Scene: HUMAN is kneeling by a chair. SATAN and GOD are standing on either side of him.

SATAN   Remember last year when you promised to go out with your aunt? And then you didn't go 'cos you felt tired.

HUMAN   Yes?

SATAN   [*pleased*] Well . . . she died the next month, didn't she? Some kind of Christian you are!

HUMAN   Well . . . yes . . . but . . .

SATAN   And what about a couple of months ago when you kept that extra change the man at the checkout gave you by mistake? Not very honest eh?

HUMAN   [*sadly*] No, I know that . . .

SATAN   [*accusingly*] And then there's that juicy bit of gossip about your neighbour last week that you just couldn't keep to yourself. How many other people did you pass that on to then? Two? Three? Oh dear, you have been making a mess of things. You'd better give up on this trying to be a Christian lark. Admit it, you're just no good at it.

HUMAN   [*in despair*] Oh God! [*Looks at list of sins written down.*]

GOD	Yes? What is it?
HUMAN	Oh, you're still there.
GOD	Yes, why shouldn't I be?
HUMAN	Oh, I thought you might have gone after all this.
GOD	All what?
HUMAN	This list of my failures. [*Hands them to GOD.*] Well, some of them anyway.
GOD	I can't see any failures.
HUMAN	You can't?
GOD	No, this is what I see. [*Hands back the list.*]
HUMAN	(*reads*) 'If we confess our sins to God he will keep his promise and do what is right; he will forgive us our sins and cleanse us from all our wrongdoing.' [*Tentatively*] I forgot, yes, I did say 'sorry' for all those things, didn't I?
GOD	Yes, you did. Now read the next part.
HUMAN	[*reads*] 'The Lord is merciful and loving, slow to become angry and full of constant love. He does not keep on telling us off . . . he does not punish us as we deserve . . . As far as the east is from the west that far does God remove our sins from us.' Wow! Thank you, Lord. I'm sorry I forgot how great your forgiveness is. Thank you that you wipe out my failures and keep giving me fresh starts. Thank you so much.
SATAN	[*mutter mutter, grumble grumble*] I'll be back!

J. Plumb
Dove Street

Q. Henrietta the Hen

*This story can be used at any time, but it fits particularly
well into the weeks after Easter while children's minds are
still full of thoughts of Easter eggs.*

Henrietta was a brown speckled hen. She lived on a farm
in a barn.

She had a job to do. She had laid some brown speckled
eggs and as the farm was only a small one and did not
have any special machines for hatching eggs it was her job
to sit on the eggs until they hatched.

In a way it was a rather boring job, sitting on the eggs
day after day after day. But it was her job and she was
determined to do it.

One day, a beautiful sunny morning, when the sky was
blue and the air was warm, Tom the farm cat put his head
around the barn door. He was a black cat apart from one
paw and the tip of his tail which were both white. He
rubbed himself against the barn door and said, 'Me-ow!
Henrietta, surely you have sat on those eggs long enough.
It's a lovely morning. Come and lie in the sunshine in the
farmyard with me.'

'Cluck!' said Henrietta. 'I know it is a lovely morning
and I would like to come into the farmyard with you, but I
have a job to do and I must do it.'

Some time later Patch the farm dog put his head around
the barn door. He was mostly white but he had a big brown
patch all round one eye. Patch said, 'Wuff! Henrietta,

311

surely you have sat on those eggs long enough. It's dull in here. Come and play with me in the meadow and let's have some fun.'

'Cluck!' said Henrietta. 'It is rather dull in this barn and I would very much like to play with you in the meadow, but I have a job to do and I must do it.'

The day went by and the sun rose high in the sky and it became hotter and hotter.

After a while one of the ducks came and put her head around the barn door.

'Quack!' said the duck. 'It's so hot and stuffy in here. Surely you have sat on those eggs long enough. Why not come down with me to the pond where it is cool?'

It was true. It was very hot and very stuffy. Henrietta was very tempted, but she pulled herself together and said, 'Cluck! Thank you for the invitation. I would love to come to the pond and perhaps I shall be able to soon, but just now I have a job to do and I must do it.'

One day while Tom and Patch and the duck were with Henrietta in the barn, there was a cracking sound. Henrietta stood up and they all saw that one of the eggs was beginning to crack open. Then another started to break. Then another.

It was not long before Henrietta was surrounded by little yellow chicks.

'Cheep, cheep, cheep,' said the chicks.

Tom and Patch and the duck wondered what it meant. But Henrietta knew. It meant, 'Thank you, Mummy.'

It is easy enough to start a job. The important thing is to finish it. Sir Francis Drake wrote a prayer about this:

O Lord God, when thou givest to thy servants to endeavour any great matter, grant us also to know that it is not the beginning, but the continuing of the same, until it be thoroughly finished, which yieldeth the true glory; through him that for the finishing of thy work laid down his life, our Redeemer, Jesus Christ. Amen.

Roy Lawrence
Prenton, Merseyside

R. The Upside-Down Men

Have you ever tried drawing upside-down men? It's a good game. What you have to do is to draw a face which looks all right when it's the right way up, but looks even better when you turn it upside down.

For instance, there's this man with a beard.

When you turn him upside down, he hasn't got a beard. He has a party hat on instead.

Or there's this funny looking fellow.

When you turn him upside down he is just as surprised as you are!

But here's the one I want you to look at particularly today.

He's a miserable looking customer, and the only way to make him look happy is to turn him upside down.

The reason why he is worth thinking about is that in a way the whole human race is like him.

On the whole we put ourselves first and don't think much about Jesus. Because of this the world is full of selfishness and this causes injustice and war and all sorts of misery.

We talk a lot about wanting everybody to be happy, but if we are ever going to manage it we are going to have to turn ourselves upside down. Instead of putting ourselves first and not thinking much about Jesus, we must put Jesus first and not think so much about ourselves. That's the way to bring happiness into the world.

When I was a boy someone told me that to spell JOY you put J for Jesus first, O for others next and Y for yourself last of all, and the result is JOY. And it's true.

It's not easy. There's a lot in our life that we have to turn upside down before we come anywhere near to it, but it's the true way to happiness.

Roy Lawrence
Prenton, Merseyside

S. Jasper, Caspar and George

Once upon a time there were three princes, Jasper, Caspar and George. They lived in a vast palace with their father, the old king.

Their father was very old indeed and he knew that soon he would have to hand over his throne to one of his sons. But he just could not decide which one of his sons should be king after him.

In the end he decided he would set the three princes a test.

One morning the king summoned his sons before him in the throne room. They stood in a row and bowed their heads before him.

Their father looked at them in silence for a while, and then said, 'I am going to set you a test to decide which of you shall be king after me.'

He put his hand into a bag which hung at his waist and brought out three gold pieces. He gave one to each prince.

'Go into my kingdom,' he said, 'and with these gold pieces buy something which will fill this entire palace. Remember you must be back before nightfall. Whoever is the first to fill the whole palace shall be king after me.'

This was a very hard task because it was a vast palace with lots of big rooms and long passages.

Jasper, the first prince, lost no time in starting. He jumped on his horse and galloped off to the nearest market.

He stopped in front of a trader.

316

'What is the cheapest thing for sale in this market?' he called.

'Well, Sire,' answered the trader, 'beans are cheap this year, and potatoes are even cheaper. But I suppose the cheapest thing of all is straw. But who would want to buy straw?'

Prince Jasper flipped the gold piece to him.

'Pile your wagon high with straw, merchant,' he said, 'and bring it to the palace. I want as much straw as I can possibly have for that gold piece.'

The merchant was anxious to please and piled two wagons high with straw and sent them to the palace.

But both wagon-loads could have fitted into one corner of the big throne room and so Jasper failed the test.

Caspar heard of his brother's failure and said to himself 'I must do better than that.'

He rode his horse far beyond the market town into the countryside where money was scarce and a gold piece would be worth a great deal.

He stopped in a village and asked a villager, 'What is cheaper to buy in this village than straw?'

'Well, Sire,' said the villager, 'straw is very, very cheap indeed in this village. But mud is cheaper still. We have heaps of mud all over the village. We would be very pleased to be rid of it.'

Prince Caspar flipped his gold piece to the villager.

'Load up all the wagons you can find with mud and have it delivered to the palace,' he said. And he rode back to the palace to wait for the mud to be delivered.

Early in the afternoon along came ten big wagons loaded with mud. The villagers emptied the mud—slurp, slurp, slurp—in large heaps in the courtyard of the palace. But there was not enough to fill even the throne room of the palace, and the king was very cross, because his courtyard had been made so dirty. So Caspar failed the test.

'It's impossible,' said Caspar to Jasper. 'Nothing is cheaper than mud.' And they both agreed that George hadn't a chance.

George felt very depressed when he heard how difficult his brothers had found the test. He rode his horse up and down long roads and lanes, in and out of towns and villages. It all seemed impossible. The night was drawing near and it was becoming darker. Then suddenly he had an idea. He went into a shop and came out with a parcel. Then he galloped as hard as he could for the palace.

His brothers were surprised to see him arrive with no more than a parcel, but he took his parcel straight into the throne room and opened it on the floor.

Inside were hundreds of penny candles.

He lit a dozen in the throne room and two or three in every other room or passage.

They were only little candles but they filled the palace—with light.

And so George passed the test, and he became the next king.

Each prince had a gold piece. One spent it on worthless straw. One spent it on messy mud. One spent it bringing light into a dark place. Think for a moment—every man's life is like a gold piece. We can spend our lives doing things that are worthless. We can spend our lives doing things that are messy and destructive. Or we can spend our lives trying to bring light into a dark world.

When the world seems dark and sad we can try to light the candle of happiness. When the world seems dark and cruel we can try to light the candle of kindliness.

God our Father wants us to inherit his wonderful kingdom. But everyone who is going to inherit the kingdom of God must first be a candle-lighter in his own way.

That is why Jesus says to us, 'Let your light shine out before men.'

Roy Lawrence
Prenton, Merseyside

T. The Story of the Two People Who Went to Church

ONE   One day Jesus was with his friends,

TWO   Peter, James, John and the rest of them.

ONE   There were other people around as well, who were talking to one another.

TWO   Jesus could not help hearing what they were saying

ONE   and he was not very pleased with what they were saying.

TWO   It sounded as though they were criticising everyone else, but they thought that they themselves were rather good.

ONE   You may have done the same thing yourself, just occasionally.

TWO   Jesus decided he would tell them a story

ONE   to make them think,

TWO   to make us think.

ONE   It went something like this:

TWO   (We are telling the story as Jesus might tell us today,

ONE   to help us understand better.)

TWO   One day two people went to church to pray,

ONE   one was a vicar,

TWO   The Reverend I am Good

ONE   Ian Good, you mean.

       [*Mr Good enters church and walks to the Chancel steps with great confidence.*]

TWO   The other was Miss Verity Dodgy

ONE   She had been thrown out of Priory School.

TWO   Something to do with stealing and possibly drugs.

ONE   She now ran the betting shop,

TWO   when she was not appearing in court.

ONE   She also went into church that day.
       [*Miss Dodgy enters church and walks rather
       uncertainly to the middle of the central aisle.*]

TWO   Mr Good climbed the pulpit steps [*Mr Good
       climbs steps*]

ONE   looked up to God

TWO   and began to pray.

ONE   At least he spoke to himself, if not to God.

TWO   'Thank you, God,

ONE   that I am not like other people.

TWO   They all make a mess of their lives.

ONE   I see them every day:

TWO   thieves,

ONE   law breakers,

TWO   unfaithful,

ONE   rotten through and through.

TWO   No wonder the country is in such a state.'

ONE   Mr Good then looked down and saw Verity,

TWO   so he continued speaking.

ONE   'Thank goodness I am not like that woman over
       there.

TWO   I am surprised that she dares to come into your
       house, Lord.'

ONE   'You know, Lord, how well I am doing,' Mr Good
       continued.

TWO   'I come to church every Sunday,

ONE   and I put a lot in the collection.

TWO   I never do anyone any harm,

ONE   in fact I live up to my name.'

TWO   Verity was behaving very differently.

ONE	She did not want anyone to notice her.
TWO	She bowed her head in shame
ONE	and kept on saying,
TWO	'God, please forgive me. I am an absolute failure.
ONE	Please forgive me. I have done so many wrong things.
TWO	Please forgive me. Please be merciful to me.'
ONE	Mr Good then came down from the pulpit and returned home.
TWO	He felt that he was all right.
ONE	Verity also left for her home.
TWO	She wondered if God had heard her.
ONE	But she felt a kind of peace, which she had never known before.
TWO	Jesus said,
ONE	It was Verity Dodgy who went home right with God,
TWO	not Ian Good.
ONE	You see those who think themselves better than others,
TWO	are seen by God as they really are.
ONE	But those who know themselves as they really are
TWO	and who know how much they have failed God,
ONE	receive God's forgiveness and a place in his family.
TWO	Those who heard Jesus' story were amazed.
ONE	Could it really be true that Miss Dodgy was nearer to God than Mr Good?
TWO	The people went home wondering what this meant for them.

INTERVIEW WITH THE REVD IAN GOOD

Why did you come to church today?
Well, I always go to church. It is a good thing to do.

What did you think of Miss Verity Dodgy?
Who? Oh, you mean the girl from the betting shop. I was surprised to see her in church. I am not sure that it is a good thing when people like her come to church.

What did you feel as you went home afterwards?
Fine: I had reported to my boss how well I had been getting on.

What do you think about yourself? How do you see yourself?
I think I am lucky. I find it easy to live a good life. I can understand why God loves me.

What do you imagine that God is like?
Well, I think he must be pleased with me, but I can't understand how he lets most people go on living in the way that they do.

We understand that Jesus said that Miss Dodgy went home right with God and that you didn't. What do you think about that?
What absolute cheek! I have never heard such rubbish in all my life. I am sure you've got it wrong. I must be off. I am a busy man, you know.

INTERVIEW WITH MISS VERITY DODGY

Why did you come to church today?
I don't really know. I felt so desperate about myself and the life I was living, that I wanted to try to make a fresh start.

What did you think of the Revd Ian Good?
Who? Was there someone else in the church? I didn't notice anyone else there.

What did you feel as you went home afterwards?

A sense of great relief. Somehow I felt clean. I don't know why, but I felt that I had gone in there dirty and been washed clean.

What do you think about yourself? How do you see yourself?
I know that I have not been the kind of person that I should have been. I have failed myself, and I have failed other people as well, specially those who love me.

What do you imagine that God is like?
I remember once being told that God is like the best father you could ever have. I imagine that you could always turn to him when you need help, and that if you want to be different he will help you.

We understand that Jesus said that you went home right with God and that Mr Good didn't. What do you think about that?
If that is true, I think it's amazing. I can hardly believe that God forgives me and accepts me after all the things that I have done wrong. What a wonderful person he must be. I must go and tell a friend of mine about him. Bye.

(It is better if you do not try to learn the answers to the questions off by heart or read them out. Rather, try to answer the questions as you think your character might answer them. I have written down a possible answer, and if your answer can be something like that this would be helpful.)

Peter Markby
Lewes

U.   An Old Roman Story

There is an old Roman story which tells how a Roman emperor was enjoying a triumph. He had the privilege, which Rome gave to her great victors, of marching his troops through the streets of Rome, with all his captured trophies and his prisoners in his train. So the Emperor was on the march with his troops. The streets were lined with cheering people. The tall legionaries lined the streets' edges to keep the people in their places. At one point on the triumphal route there was a little platform where the Empress and her family were sitting to watch the Emperor go by in all the pride of his triumph. On the platform with his mother there was the Emperor's youngest son, a little boy. As the Emperor came near the little boy he jumped off the platform, burrowed through the crowd, tried to dodge between the legs of a legionary, and to run out to the road to meet his father's chariot. The legionary stooped down and stopped him. He swung him up in his arms: 'You can't do that, boy,' he said. 'Don't you know who that is in the chariot? That's the Emperor. You can't run out to his chariot.' And the little lad laughed. 'He may be your Emperor,' he said, 'but he's my father.'

That is exactly the way Christians feel towards God. The might, and the majesty, and the power are the might and the majesty and the power of one whom Jesus Christ taught us to call 'our Father'.

(Taken from *Daily Readings in Matthew* by William Barclay.)

V.   The Influence of the Bible

In the year 1787 one of His Majesty's transport ships sailed from Spithead. Captain Bligh was the captain, and the ship was the *Bounty*. On board were between twenty and thirty sailors. Captain Bligh was pretty rough on them. He was a very strict disciplinarian. They sailed for the South Seas to collect bread fruit trees, but when they landed at Tahiti, they found a veritable paradise. Not only did they find wonderful blue seas and golden sands, but they found the most glamorous girls that sailors ever dreamed about. Soon every sailor had his girlfriend, and to their great delight they stayed there several months. When Captain Bligh eventually announced that the next day they were setting sail, he was not very popular. Fletcher Christian started mumbling and complaining and talking secretly to some of the men about mutiny and staying there at Tahiti for the rest of their lives, and getting rid of Captain Bligh and the *Bounty*.

However, they sailed, but a few days out old Captain Bligh woke up one morning and found himself looking into the barrel of a gun. Fletcher Christian and the eight mutineers on board headed the ship back to Tahiti. When they got back, without difficulty they persuaded not eight but twelve girls to go on board with them, and they headed back to sea. They had no plans, but after sailing for some time, frightened in case they would be overtaken, they came across Pitcairn Island—an extinct volcano and a beautiful place. There were no sands, but steep cliffs, and luscious vegetation. They went ashore and found no one living there, so they moved everything they could from on board and set fire to the *Bounty*, and watched her sink beneath the waves.

Then they turned round for 'paradise on earth', but actually it was ten years of hell that they faced. One of the men with the old copper kettle from the *Bounty*, rigged up a distillery, and they distilled the roots of the trees, and started to make spirits. Before long the sailors and the women were incapable. They lived that way for days, weeks, months on end. Some of the men went mad and became like beasts. One flung himself over the cliff. They fought among themselves. After several years, there were only two men left, Edward Young and Alexander Smith. Young was an older man, ill with asthma. The women, with the eighteen children that had been born to them, one night seized the firearms and barricaded themselves in. The two remaining sailors lived alone. Neither the children nor the women would go near them. Young knew that he was dying. One day he went to the ship's chest, and at the bottom among the papers he found a book—old, bound in leather, somewhat mildewed and worm-eaten. He lifted it out. He had not read for years. The book he held in his hand was the *Bounty's* Bible.

He began at Genesis, chapter 1. His friend Lex could not read a word, so he taught him to read. The two men, frightened and disillusioned, utter wrecks, together read the Bible. They read through Genesis, Exodus, Leviticus, Numbers, and as they read both knew that God was holy and they were sinful. They did their best to pray. They read on, seeking for help and light, in the Old Testament.

The little children were the first to come back, because they noticed the change in the men. The children brought the women back, and they used to sit down and listen while Edward Young and sometimes Smith, the younger man, spelt out the words to them. When they came to the Psalms they realised that this was some sort of hymn book, and in their quaint way they started to sing the Psalms of David.

One tragic night Young died. When Smith came to the New Testament, a lovely thing happened. He said, 'I had been working like a mole for years, and suddenly it was as if the doors flew wide open, and I saw the light, and I met God in Jesus Christ. And the burden of my sin rolled away, and I found new life in Christ.'

Eighteen years after the Mutiny of the *Bounty* a ship from Boston came across the island and the captain landed. He found a community of men and young people who were quiet and godly, with a grace and peace about them that he had never seen before. Their leader stepped forward, 'My name is Alexander Smith. I am the only remaining member of the ship's company of the *Bounty*. If you want to give me up, you may.'

'I know nothing about that,' said the captain. 'All I know is that these people here need you.' When he got back to the Unites States he reported that in all his travels he had never seen or met with a people who were so good, so gracious, so loving. How did that happen? There is only one book in the world that would produce a miracle like that.

(Taken from *Can Intelligent People Believe?* by Tom Rees.)

W. Except the Lord Build the House...

At the American Constitutional Convention in 1787 delegates from the thirteen States of the Union had spent two months trying to thrash out an agreement. Independence had been won from the English, but the peace was proving to be difficult as each state vied for its own interests.

Benjamin Franklin, then in his eighties, looked at the chaos in the assembly and asked permission to speak. The scientist, rationalist and philosopher leaned on his cane, peered through the spectacles pinched on the end of his nose and addressed the assembly.

'How has it happened, sir, that we have not hitherto once thought of humbly applying to the Father of Lights to illuminate our understanding? In the beginning of the contest with Britain, when we were sensible of danger, we had daily prayers in this room for Divine protection. Our prayers, sir, were heard, and they were graciously answered. . . Do we imagine we no longer need His assistance?

'I have lived, sir, a long time, and the longer I live, the more convincing proofs I see of this truth: "that God governs in the affairs of men", and if a sparrow cannot fall to the ground without His notice, is it probable that an empire can rise without His aid?

'We have been assured, sir, in the sacred writings that except the Lord build the house, they labour in vain that build it. I firmly believe this. I also believe that, without

His concurring aid, we shall succeed in this political building no better than the builders of Babel: we shall be divided by our little, partial, local interests; our projects will be confounded; and we ourselves shall become a reproach and a by-word down to future ages.'

He then went on to move a motion that prayers should precede each day's deliberations. Not one of the delegates was prepared to second the motion. The Convention went on prayerlessly to enact a constitution which would fudge the issue of slavery and thereby ensure a bloody Civil War.

Franklin had, like Nebuchadnezzar of Babylon, learned that 'The Most High God is sovereign over the kingdoms of men and gives them to anyone he wishes' (Daniel 4: 32).

Because we do not see His hand, that does not alter His headship of powers on earth or in the heavenlies. Whether president or poltergeist, senate or spirit, government or ghost, minister or medium, all come under one authority but not all are part of His body, the Church.

(Taken from *Good Morning, Disciple* by Vic Jackopson, published by Marshall Pickering and used by permission.)

X. It Is True

A Russian Army captain came to a minister in Hungary and asked to see him alone. The boy was very young and brash, and very conscious of his role as conquerer. When he had been led to a small conference room and the door was closed, he nodded towards the cross that hung on the wall.

'You know that thing is a lie,' he said to the minister. 'It's just a piece of trickery you ministers use to delude the poor people to make it easier for the rich to keep them ignorant. Come now, we are alone! Admit to me that you never really believed that Jesus Christ was the Son of God!'

The minister smiled. 'But, my poor young man, of course I believe it. It is true.'

'I won't have you play these tricks on me!' cried the captain. 'This is serious. Don't laugh at me!'

He drew out his revolver and held it close to the body of the minister.

'Unless you admit to me that it is a lie, I'll fire!'

'I cannot admit that, for it is not true. Our Lord is really and truly the Son of God,' said the minister.

The captain flung his revolver on the floor and embraced the man of God. Tears sprang to his eyes.

'It *is true*!' he cried. '*It is true*, I believe so too, but I could not be sure men would die for this belief until I found it out for myself. Oh, thank you! You have

331

strengthened my faith. Now I too can die for Christ. You have shown me how.'

(Taken from *Tortured for Christ* by Richard Wurmbrand, published by Hodder and Stoughton and used by permission.)

Y. William Tyndale

(Originally written for a service in Chester Cathedral to commemorate the 500th anniversary of the birth of William Tyndale.) The sketch should take place around the singing of the hymn by Christopher Idle 'How sure the Scriptures are!' (see *Hymns for Today's Church* 249, recommended tune: Darwell's 148th, HTC 171).

Cast and costume

Narrator, who can also help make small adjustments to the set during the singing of the verses of the hymn. He should be dressed in black.

Tyndale should have a black close-fitting cap and beard. Initially he should wear a good quality academic gown, but underneath an inferior black gown and beneath that an old long shirt.

Staging and props

At the back an upright pole to represent a stake with some straw or faggots in front. It is very effective if a red light can be concealed behind these.

Front stage there should be a chair and table with some paper, a small ink bottle and a quill pen, or large feather to represent one. Candle and matches. Some large old well-bound books.

Before the hymn starts the narrator explains: 'We are now going to have four quotations from the lips of

William Tyndale around the three verses of hymn [give number]. Please remain seated throughout.'

Narrator: Tyndale was brought up from a child in the University of Oxford and enrolled as a student at Magdalen Hall in about 1505. (*Enter Tyndale, who sits at the table and picks up quill.*) He had no enthusiasm for the study prescribed. He wrote:

Episode 1 (*Tyndale seated at a table writing*)

Tyndale: In the universities they have ordained that no man shall look on the Scriptures until he be noselled in heathen learning eight or nine years, and armed with false principles with which he is clean shut out of the understanding of the Scriptures.

Hymn verse 1 'How sure the Scriptures are!'

Episode 2 (*Tyndale seated at table writing. Old books have been piled around*)

Tyndale: I perceive by experience how that it was impossible to establish the lay people in any truth, except the Scriptures were plainly laid before their eyes in their mother tongue. (*He stands, and as if addressing an opponent*) If God spare my life, ere many years pass, I will cause a boy that driveth the plough shall know more of the Scriptures than thou dost.

Hymn verse 2 'They test each human thought . . .'

Episode 3 (*Tyndale without academic gown and looking dishevelled sits at the table with old books piled around. He is writing slowly by candle light.*)

Narrator: Realising that it was becoming too dangerous to

pursue his translation work in England, Tyndale fled to Northern Europe in May 1524 to complete his work on the New Testament and later on parts of the Old Testament.

Tyndale: In the begynnynge was that worde/and that worde was with god: and god was thatt worde. The same was in the begynnynge wyth god. All thyngs were made by it/and without it/was made noo thinge/that made was. In it was life. . . (*Candle is blown out.*)

Hymn verse 3 'Let those who hear his voice . . .'
(*During this verse table and chair are removed from set.*)

Episode 4 (*Tyndale, dressed in an old shirt, stands against the upright post with rope attached, which also goes round his neck.*)

Narrator: For most of his years in Europe Tyndale was hounded by the religious authorities, accused of being a heretic. He was eventually caught, tried, and on 6th October 1536 let out to meet his death at the stake.

Tyndale: (*Looking up to heaven and crying loudly and with fervour*) Lord, open the King of England's eyes! (*The red light below him is switched on— there is a short silence.*)

Michael Botting
Editor

APPENDIX 2
Resources

Sources for drama

Bell, John and Maule, Graham. *Sketches from the Iona Community*: 1. Life and teaching of Jesus. 2. Death and forgiveness: Jesus answers questions. 3. Old Testament. 4. Lent and Easter. 5. Parables of Jesus and Paul. 6. Advent and Christmas. Wild Goose Publications.
Eh, Jesus. . . Yes, Peter. . . ? Volumes 1–3. (Dialogues between Jesus and Peter, where Peter is asking most of the questions.) Wild Goose Publications.

Botting, Michael. *Drama for all the Family*. Kingsway, 1993.

Burbridge, Paul and Watts, Murray. *A Time to Act*. Hodder and Stoughton, 1979.
Lightning Sketches. Hodder and Stoughton, 1981.
Red Letter Days. Hodder and Stoughton, 1986.
Divine Comedies. Monarch, 1994.

Cooling, Margaret. *Ten Minute Miracle Plays*. Bible Society, 1995.

Haylock, Derek. *Acts for Apostles*. National Society/ Church House Publishing, 1987.
Drama for Disciples. National Society/Church House Publishing, 1988.
Plays on the Word. National Society/Church House Publishing, 1993.
Sketches from Scripture. National Society/Church House Publishing, 1992.

Hopwood, Dave. *Child's Play; Short and Snappy; Stage Right*. All available from Christ Church, Church Street East, Woking, Surrey GU21 1YG.
Acting Up. National Society/Church House Publishing, 1995.
Jeffrey, Graham. *The Gospel According to Barnabas*. Mowbray, 1975. Other 'Barnabas' material from Palm Tree Press Ltd, 55 Leigh Road, Leigh-on-Sea, Essex.
Perry, Michael. *The Dramatised Bible*. Marshall Pickering/Bible Society, 1989.
Powell, Paul. *Scenes and Wonders*. National Society/Church House Publishing, 1994.
Watts, Murray. *Laughter in Heaven*. Marc Europe, 1985.

Books relating to drama

Forde, Nigel. *Theatrecraft*. Marc Europe, 1986.
Kelso, Andy. *Drama in Worship*. Grove Books, 1975.
Simmonds, Paul. *Reaching the Unchurched*. Grove Books, 1992.
Smith, Judy Gittis. *Show Me!* Bible Society.
Stevenson, Geoffrey. *Steps of Faith*. (On mime.) Kingsway, 1984.
Stickley, Steve and MacDonald, Alan. *The Drama Recipe Book*. Minstrel, 1989.
(with Hawthorn, Philip) *Street Theatre*. Minstrel, 1991.
Stickley, Steve and Janet. *Footnotes*. Hodder and Stoughton, 1987.
(with Jim Belben) *Using the Bible in Drama*. Bible Society, 1980.
Thompson, Ann. *In on the Act*. NCEC, 1986.
Watts, Murray. *Christianity and the Theatre*. Handsel, 1986.

Sources for prayers

Botting, Michael. *Prayers for all the Family*. Kingsway, 1993.

Colquhoun, Frank (ed). *Contemporary Parish Prayers*. Hodder and Stoughton.
New Parish Prayers. Hodder and Stoughton.

Knox, Ian. . . . *And All the Children Said Amen*. Scripture Union, 1994.

Perry, Michael (ed). *Biblical Praying*. Fount.
Church Family Worship. Hodder and Stoughton.

Simmonds, Paul (ed). *Church Family Worship Resource Book*. Church Pastoral Aid Society.

Williams, Dick (ed). *More Prayers for Today's Church*. Kingsway, 1986.

General books relating to family services

Backhouse, Robert (ed). *1500 Illustrations for Preaching and Teaching*. Marshall Pickering, 1991.

Brierley, Peter. *Reaching and Keeping Teenagers*. Marc, 1993.

Cray, Jackie. *Seen and Heard: Valuing Children in Your Church*. Monarch, 1995.

Croft, Ann. *Children in Creches and Toddler Groups*. Church Pastoral Aid Society, 1995.

Dean, Margaret (ed). *Pick and Mix*. National Society/ Church House Publishing, 1992.
Learning and Worship Ideas for All Ages. National Society/Church House Publishing.

Finney, John. *Finding Faith Today*. Bible Society, 1992.

Frank, Penny and Stroud, Marion. *The Journey Parents Make*. Church Pastoral Aid Society, 1994.

Swain, Sharon. *The Sermon Slot: Ideas for All-Age Worship*. SPCK, 1992.

Winnicott, D.W. *The Child, the Family and the Outside World*. Pelican.

The Church of England Board of Social Responsibility Working Party report 'Something to Celebrate: Valuing Families in Church and Society'. Church House Publishing, 1995. Summary and Guide also available from Church House Bookshop, Great Smith Street, London SW1P 3BN. Minority addition (by Dr Alan Storkey, lecturer in sociology at Oak Hill Theological College and formerly a member of the Working Party until 1995) available from the General Synod Office, Church House, Great Smith Street, London SW1P 3NZ.

(The Editor does not support the liberal views on sexual relationships expressed in this book. However, the book does include the results of considerable research on all aspects of family life today, and the contribution which the church should be making to support it.)

Equipment and audio-visual aids

See the Appendix to *More for all the Family* by Michael Botting (Kingsway, 1990).

For information and advice on overhead projectors, see *Teaching the Family* by Michael Botting (Kingsway, 1994), pp 39–43.

For staging in church see *Drama for all the Family* by Michael Botting (Kingsway, 1993), p 19. Budget Direct plc, catalogue D21 for church products also recommend staging on pages VI and 20 of their 1995 edition. If this is not easily obtainable, call Budget free on 0800 282814.

Family Service material on computer

The E-text Co-op is a forum for exchange of church orientated texts on computer disk. The material available depends entirely on contributions members are able to make. At present there is a very large selection of prayers of all sorts, outline services, including family services, and general material such as hints and tips for intercession leaders.

Membership is £8.00 plus at least one original contribution per year.

New members get virtually the whole current collection straight away.

Further details from the Revd Bob Emm, The Rectory, Church Lane, North Thoresby, Grimsby DN36 5QG. Tel: 01472 840029.

Scripture Index

Subject Index